Series / Number 07-077

EXPERT SYSTEMS

ROBERT A. BENFER
University of Missouri — Columbia

EDWARD E. BRENT, JR.
University of Missouri — Columbia

LOUANNA FURBEE
University of Missouri — Columbia

BNJO

SAGE PUBLICATIONS
The International Professional Publishers
Newbury Park   London   New Delhi

For information address:

SAGE Publications, Inc.
2455 Teller Road
Newbury Park, California 91320

SAGE Publications Ltd.
6 Bonhill Street
London EC2A 4PU
United Kingdom

SAGE Publications India Pvt. Ltd.
M-32 Market
Greater Kailash I
New Delhi 110 048 India

Printed in the United States of America

International Standard Book Number 0-8039-4036-X

Library of Congress Catalog Card No. 90-8731

FIRST PRINTING, 1991

Sage Production Editor: Judith L. Hunter

When citing a university paper, please use the proper form. Remember to cite the current Sage University Paper series title and include the paper number. One of the following formats can be adapted (depending on the style manual used):

(1) WELLER, S. C., & ROMNEY, A. K. (1990) Metric Scaling: Correspondence Analysis. Sage University Paper Series on Quantitative Applications in the Social Sciences, 07-075. Newbury Park, CA: Sage.

OR

(2) Weller, S. C., & Romney, A. K. (1990). *Metric scaling: Correspondence analysis* (Sage University Paper series on Quantitative Applications in the Social Sciences, series no. 07-075). Newbury Park, CA: Sage.

CONTENTS

SERIES EDITOR'S INTRODUCTION

An *expert system* is a computer program designed to act like a human expert in a specific area of knowledge. Programming languages from artifical intelligence (AI) work, such as LISP and PROLOG, or expert system "shells," are commonly employed (althought they could be written in standard languages such as FORTRAN). In their excellent monograph, Benfer, Brent, and Furbee offer numerous insightful examples. The first, called "MUckraker," consists of a program developed to guide investigative reporters. As with most expert systems, it is rule based. For instance, a series of **If, Then** rules prompt the reporter-user, leading to a conclusion about the best way to contact the news source.

The typical expert system has four parts: the knowledge base, the inference "engine," the knowledge-acquisition interface, and the user interface. When the system is properly constructed, it behaves as a highly informed "insider" within its narrow knowledge domain, interacting with the user to arrive at a decision. In a well-chosen, recurring example, the authors construct an expert system for soil classification and crop choice regarding farmland in the Peruvian Andes.

Such construction work may not be easy. We are told, rightly: "Intelligent expert systems are not created overnight." An obvious difficulty involves discovery of the many rules, formal and informal, that the expert really follows. Benfer and colleagues meet this obstacle with sensitivity and ingenuity, offering numerous strategies such as decision trees and flow charts for acquiring an accurate, manageable knowledge base. Further, a descriptive, up-to-date list of available expert systems programs is provided in the Appendix.

The authors point out that the technique, with its emphasis on rules or equations to formalize relationships among empirical observations, fits comfortably into the scientific tradition. Importantly, they spell out the many social science applications. For instance, key propositions in Simmel's conflict theory have been effectively translated into formal AI programming language. In research design, the approach has been applied to the determination of sample size. It has been used to simulate President John F. Kennedy's decision in the Cuban Missile Crisis. In addition to these examples, others are offered in the areas of theory development and testing, data collection and analysis, cognitive modeling, teaching, and public service delivery. Those interested in acquiring an appreciation of expert systems, as well as those wishing to utilize the method, will find the necessary ingredients with this outstanding volume.

Michael S. Lewis-Beck
Series Editor

1

PREFACE

This book introduces the process of expert systems development as a model for acquiring, representing, and validating knowledge about relatively limited domains of human behavior. Many of the examples derive from the authors' own development experiences in the social sciences, with both normative and descriptive modeling systems.

At first glance, the relationship between expert systems and the social sciences might appear tenuous. Most social science applications of expert systems are recent. Even the phrase "knowledge engineering" seems to deny that development is a social process. Indeed, a recent book on elicitation of knowledge for expert systems employs the metaphor of knowledge as a natural, *mineral* resource (Bell and Hardiman, 1989), and computer scientists conducted most of the pioneering work. Psychology is generally recognized as having ideas that merit the attention of expert systems developers, but the potential contributions of the other social sciences has been largely ignored in expert systems development and research.

In contrast, we argue that the social sciences and expert systems offer much to one another. Well-established social science procedures for data collection and validation can improve expert systems development, and expert systems can benefit the social sciences by providing an important new mechanism for improving social science thinking.

Experts share some of the premises and facts of other members of their culture, but they usually hold special facts and novel assumptions in some knowledge-rich area where considerable feedback has permitted them to build on their talents. Social science methods help us understand the learning, sharing, and representation of this knowledge that is directed toward some behavioral consequence. These methods will aid knowledge engineers. The research into these methods and the process of their application will occupy knowledge scientists.

EXPERT SYSTEMS

ROBERT A. BENFER, JR.
EDWARD E. BRENT, JR.
LOUANNA FURBEE
University of Missouri—Columbia

1. ARTIFICIAL INTELLIGENCE AND EXPERT SYSTEMS

Introduction: What Are Expert Systems?

Expert systems are computer programs that perform sophisticated tasks once thought possible only for human experts. If performance were the sole criterion for labeling a program an expert system, however, many decision support systems, statistical analyses, and spreadsheet programs could be called expert systems. Instead, the term "expert system" is generally reserved for systems that achieve expert-level performance, using artificial intelligence programming techniques such as symbolic representation, inference, and heuristic search (Buchanan, 1985).[1] Knowledge-based systems can be distinguished from other branches of artificial intelligence research by their emphasis on domain-specific knowledge, rather than more general problem-solving strategies. Because their strength derives from such domain-specific knowledge rather than more general problem-solving strategies (Feigenbaum, 1977), expert systems are often called "knowledge-based." Since the knowledge of experts tends to be domain-specific rather than general, most expert systems representing this knowledge reflect the specialized nature of such expertise.

These points are illustrated by some examples of social science expert systems that we have developed.

- MUckraker, an expert system under development by New Directions in News and the Investigative Reporters and Editors Association at Missouri University, is a program to advise investigative reporters on how to approach people for interviews, how to prepare for those interviews, and how to examine a wide range of public documents in the conduct of an investigation. This program is designed to act much as an expert investigative reporter might, advising the user on strategies to try when sources are reluctant to be interviewed, pointing out documents that might be relevant to the investigation, and advising the user on how to organize his or her work.

- STATISTICAL NAVIGATOR™ is an expert system that advises users on which forms of statistical analysis to use in empirical research. It asks users a series of questions about research objectives and assumptions, then uses their responses to identify the analyses most suitable to their problem. STATISTICAL NAVIGATOR™ performs the role of a teacher or statistical consultant to advise the user on the selection of statistics, to explain why one technique is better than another, and to help the user learn the criteria to apply in making those decisions.

- AI-MOMS predicts when a mother-to-be will seek prenatal care based on her feelings about a variety of issues related to maternity and the circumstances of her pregnancy. This qualitative information is used to make the qualitative prediction of whether the expectant mother will seek prenatal care early or late. In this instance, there is a public policy implication since mothers-to-be who seek prenatal care late in their pregnancies have much larger hospital bills and less good outcomes for the pregnancy than those who seek care earlier (Fisher et al., 1988).

Before writing the AI-MOMS prototype, data from the mothers-to-be were analyzed using multiple dummy regression to predict the week of pregnancy at which the woman would first present herself for prenatal care. The model was effective; the multiple R^2 was above .7 (McKinney, 1987). However, these women did not compute weighted sums of the values of dummy variables in order to decide when first to seek medical care. Instead, they probably followed some rules, or rules of thumb. An expert system proved able to predict successfully whether a woman would seek prenatal care early or late in her pregnancy (Benfer, 1988). The model was constructed of only a few simple rules of the sort

If there is support from a family member
Then present late.

This rule was not anticipated, but in reviewing the written interviews, we found that when mothers or other important relatives of the mother-to-be encouraged the woman to believe that the pregnancy was normal and healthy, the women tended to seek prenatal care late. Rules such as these have the additional advantage over regression studies of being easy to communicate to referring family physicians and to the general population of women at risk for pregnancy.

- AI-FORENS (Benfer et al., 1990) is an expert system that estimates the age at time of death and the sex of a skeleton from the innominate bone. It offers an example of an expert system that has both qualitative and quantitative features and involves models from different experts. Although indicators of the sex of an individual are expressed quantitatively in the human pelvis, for purposes of law enforcement use, an estimate of male or female must be made. Age at time of death is quantitative.

In this project, three forensic experts provided the knowledge bases for the three different expert systems that comprise AI-FORENS. The three experts followed somewhat different strategies for identifying an innominate as to age and sex. One employed many different procedures and stated that he attended to all logical combinations; the actual number (in the thousands) would have made for an extremely complex expert system. Instead of having one rule for each possible combination, we employed an index variable, which weighted the values from three separate lists according to the degree of confidence the expert had in their members. Another expert used fewer characteristics and attended carefully to disagreement among indicators. Thus we see that complex kinds of data, from very different sources, can be integrated naturally using an expert system.

Table 1.1 presents five simplified rules from MUckraker that illustrate this integration. In this example, variables such as send_by_mail are given numerical values; the value of the variable send_by_mail obtained by Rule 1 is manipulated in Rule 5. We usually prefer this procedure over ones built into expert system shells for manipulating *confidence factors* see Chapter 4).

Reading the rules in Table 1.1, we can trace a simple example from the "Getting in the Door" module. Here the goal is to determine whether to request an interview by mail or by telephone. The program will see that the answer lies in the conclusion of Rule 5; if the variable send_by_mail$_i$ has a value greater than 79, then one should request the interview by mail. The program examines other rules that, if true (i.e., if the If section is satisfied), could arrive at such a number and finds that Rule 2 has that capability. If the program does not possess the knowledge needed to evaluate Rule 2, perhaps from a data base of characteristics of sources, it will ask the user the first two questions in Rule 2. If the answer to both is yes, MUckraker will accept that sending a written request is one acceptable solution. If the answer is no, the program would next try Rule 4, and so forth. (This program also illustrates backward-chaining, which is described fully farther on.)

This example demonstrates several important features of expert systems. First, they are based on logical relations. Second, they may possess factual knowledge in a data base, either internal or perhaps accessible by modem. Third, they may include quantitative elements. Fourth, the expert system can give the user a reason for asking a question, either with the BECAUSE sentence or by reviewing the path that it has taken to that point. Finally, when an expert system lacks facts, it attempts to obtain them through a dialogue with the user, a dialogue that is often goal directed; this characteristic makes expert systems appear "human-like" to the user.

Expert systems vary in their uses. Some systems, such as MUckraker and STATISTICAL NAVIGATOR are "normative" systems providing advice on the performance of a task or appraising users of standards. Other systems, such as the AI-MOMS and

TABLE 1.1 Simplified Examples of Rules from MUckraker

Rule 1: Prefer_mail
  IF <u>unknown</u> whether source <u>will</u> talk with
    reporter on telephone
  AND the interview is critical
  AND there are ≥ 6 days to get the interview

  THEN (send_by_mail)$_1$ request = 60
  ELSE telephone request = 40
  BECAUSE may get the interview with
    a formal, written request

Rule 2: Definitely_prefer_mail
  IF <u>probable</u> source <u>will not</u> talk with reporter
    on telephone

  AND the interview is critical
  AND there are > 6 days to get the interview

  THEN (send_by_mail)$_2$ request = 80
  BECAUSE see Rule 1.

Rule 3: Telephone_anyway
  IF probable source will not talk with reporter
    on telephone
  AND if the interview is <u>not-critical</u>
  OR there are ≤ 6 days to get the interview

  THEN (send_by_mail)$_3$ request = 10
  BECAUSE there isn't time for mail
  AND telephoning worth a try.

Rule 4: Older_sources
  IF the age of the source is ≥ 49 years
  AND the interview is <u>critical</u>
  AND there are ≥ 6 days to get the
    interview

  THEN (send_by_mail)$_4$ request = 90
  BECAUSE older individual respond
    more positively to written requests.

Rule 5: Combine_Send-By_mail
  IF **maximum** of (send_by_mail)$_i$ > 79

  THEN send written request and ASK:
    Do you want to see a sample letter?
  ELSE telephoning worth a try
  BECAUSE most sources will talk
    to a reporter on the telephone.

AI-FORENS are more "descriptive." Among descriptive systems, programs like AI-MOMS and AI-FORENS are "predictive" while others simply describe or classify events with no intention to predict (an example of an explanatory or classification system is AI-SOILS, discussed in the following chapters). Expert systems can also be distinguished by the strategies they use for representing and reasoning about knowledge. Programs such as MUckraker and AI-MOMS are purely "qualitative," relying solely on symbolic reasoning. Other programs, such as Statistical Navigator and AI-FORENS, are also "quantitative," using qualitative symbolic reasoning in conjunction with numerical computation. STATISTICAL NAVIGATOR, for example, uses a numeric algorithm based on pattern matching to supplement its symbolic reasoning.

Kinds of Knowledge

A vernacular but useful understanding of "knowledge" is one that can be informally defined as "cognizance that derives from acquisition or familiarity gained by experience." The two major components of knowledge (in a declarative representation) are *propositions* and *spatial images* (Anderson, 1983: 23). Propositions are operationalized as rules in expert systems, whereas spatial images or patterns may be captured by statistical procedures (e.g., regression, multidimensional scaling, etc.). These statistical procedures can motivate the selection and form of rules and their contents by leading to discovery of some of the underlying structures of the knowledge. We will consider other kinds of knowledge below, but for now this informal definition and these two components capture the sense of knowledge as it has been used in the expert system literature. In this work we will also talk about representing knowledge where propositions and spatial images of the expert cannot be assumed to be the same as that of the knowledge scientist, for example, across cultures or subcultures or where the expertise of the expert is highly arcane or individual. We also will consider epistemology more formally when we discuss expert systems as a means to organize a complex scientific formalization or research project requiring management of many elements.

Expert systems are most successful when they treat only limited domains. Even in a very simple "world," such as one comprised of a few three-dimensional objects (Winograd, 1972), it is still difficult to provide a method for manipulating these objects. What has to be objectified is that knowledge of the "world" of the objects important for manipulations: for example, spheres cannot be stacked on tetrahedrons. An expert in some activity has, by definition, reduced the world's complexity by his or her specialization. Nonetheless, such knowledge is difficult to capture from the expert for at least two reasons. First, much of the knowledge lies outside direct conscious awareness; direct reporting of mental processes won't always help us construct a knowledge model. Fortunately, formal methods developed in linguistics, anthropology, and psychology can help us learn this knowledge. The second problem, and perhaps the more difficult, is that one must apprehend the world view of the expert, at least in part, in order to write an expert system faithful to that expert. Participating with the expert in actual decisions is one efficient way to come to learn such assumptions. For example, the consequences of false positives or false negatives may be quite different in medicine and mechanics. The expert may ignore his or her own stated rules in certain cases where a more fundamental rule might take precedence. The precise use of Boolean operators may not be understood by the person trying to capture the knowledge without delving into the assumptions that underlie the expert's performance. To take an obvious example, "always," may really mean "in all but exceptional cases" to the expert. Or, the Boolean operators may be linguistically ambiguous. The operator "or" may be used as an exclusive ("either X or Y but not both) or inclusive (X or Y or both). Experts from other cultures, whose native language differs from the developer's, may present even greater difficulties (see Hutchins,

1980). Assuming shared assumptions is a bad way to start creating a knowledge-based representation.

Knowledge is involved in both subject matter and method in expert systems. Indeed, the expert knowledge in expert systems commonly consists of combinations of many kinds of knowledge. As a result, the term "knowledge" itself has acquired a bewildering variety of technical meanings within expert system development. First, knowledge in many domains can be said to consist of both *declarative* (factual, static, or crystallized) knowledge and *procedural* (strategic or dynamic) knowledge. Declarative knowledge is composed of concepts and various relationships among them, including taxonomic, definitional, associational, and empirical. Procedural knowledge, in contrast, typically specifies operations to perform when reasoning or attempting to solve a problem. Examples: *Declarative knowledge* — "Public records may be examined by any citizen." *Procedural knowledge* — "If a source does not wish to be publicly associated with a tip, then he can be encouraged to go 'off the record.' "

Heuristic knowledge is specialized knowledge about a phenomenon that allows someone to rule out obviously wrong solutions and focus on the more promising ones, based on useful insights, rules of thumb, or any other technique that seems to work. For example, programs might use heuristic knowledge to identify some branches of a decision tree as promising and others as less promising, in contrast to more systematic, but less efficient programs, that would exhaustively search the entire decision tree. Unlike *scientific* (e.g., algorithmic) knowledge, which is derived from principles believed to produce knowledge about which one can be certain within specified limits, heuristic knowledge claims only that it works, and perhaps only that it works some of the time. Even when heuristic knowledge does work, we may not necessarily understand how or why. Examples: *Heuristic knowledge* — "Generally, unless there are mitigating circumstances, the best sampling frame for a regional population in the United States is obtained through random digit dialing." *Algorithmic knowledge* — "The initial distribution of correct answers to a problem in a group can be computed using the binomial distribution and values for the probability of any individual having the correct solution and the number of people in the group" (Lorge and Solomon, 1960).

Public knowledge is codified knowledge easily shared and, in many cases, amenable to formal reasoning and mathematical solution. *Private* knowledge, on the other hand, consists of rules of thumb, heuristics, and experientially based knowledge that has not yet been made generally available in the literature.[2] Knowledge in any specialty tends to include both public and private components. Public knowledge tends to meet most of the knowledge claims of scientific knowledge and hence is more powerful than private knowledge and preferred over it. Often, however, such formal systematized knowledge is unavailable, and only private, as yet uncodified knowledge may be at hand for a particular problem. Even though it may not be logical, consistent, and well organized, such knowledge may perform very well. Examples: *Public Knowledge* — "City finance department files on monthly credit card and travel expenses are public documents." *Private Knowledge* — "Employees in the finance department of a city often feel responsible for proper expenditure of city funds and often will give a reporter important tips on expense accounts, city credit cards, and so forth."

Metaknowledge is knowledge about knowledge. For expert systems, metaknowledge may be knowledge about the knowledge base or knowledge about the program itself. Programs with metaknowledge can monitor their own performance to identify and eliminate rules that are never used, to locate much-used code and optimize it, and to keep track of the source of a rule or value for help in resolution of contradictions (Lenat et al., 1983). Example: *Metaknowledge*—"The generally accepted rules for crop rotation among Andean farmers do not apply when a farmer has fewer than four fields."

What anthropologists call *world knowledge*, the artificial intelligence and expert systems literature refers to as *common sense*. We prefer the former term because it reminds us that the important feature here is not reasoning but shared knowledge. World knowledge refers to the shared web of knowledge of little and big things alike that provides the framework within which we converse and think. This form of knowledge is exemplified by common verbal communication, in which much of what is said is only implied, and understanding of what is said requires a common base of shared knowledge. Example: The following brief description of events illustrates the role of world knowledge in understanding everyday social phenomena. "John sat down at the bar and winked at the waitress. The bartender grabbed him by his shirt and said loudly, 'Don't mess with my wife, Bud!' " Understanding the meaning of this description requires that the reader (or the program) understand what a "wife" is, that speaking loudly and grabbing someone by their shirt is a hostile action, and that a wink is often an effort to flirt with someone of the opposite sex.

Expert systems, like people, tend to be "expert" within relatively narrow substantive domains. Expert systems do not easily recognize when the problem they are working on is beyond the domain limits or scope of their competence (a characteristic they share with inexperienced human experts). *Domain knowledge* is the knowledge that one has about a specific domain — including assumptions and categories. It is not necessarily predictable from world knowledge, nor is the converse true. For example, deep hierarchies (those with many levels related by class inclusions) may not be characteristic of much human knowledge (Randall, 1976), but they may be employed by experts in a specific domain. Analogous knowledge may be common in the world view of many peoples, but less important in a specific domain. In any case, expert systems are representations of knowledge, representations that can be developed in a variety of ways.

Expert System Development Environments

In theory, expert systems could be constructed using almost any programming language, and some have been written using traditional computing languages such as

FORTRAN or PASCAL (e.g., EXPERT by Weiss et al., 1981). However, most expert systems are written using special languages designed for artificial intelligence such as LISP or PROLOG, or using *expert system shells—programs designed for the construction of expert systems.*

LISP, which stands for LISt Processing, is one of the oldest computer languages still in use. It was developed initially by John McCarthy at MIT in the 1950s and dominates artificial intelligence programming in the United States today. LISP is a versatile symbolic processing language that can represent diverse concepts using lists, can be programmed recursively (i.e., something can be defined in terms of itself) and can be extended by defining new functions. The classic text on LISP is Winston and Horn (1985).

PROLOG, which stands for PROgramming in LOGic, was first implemented in 1972 and is more popular than LISP in Europe and Japan. PROLOG is a nonprocedural or declarative language that permits users to solve a problem by describing what is to be accomplished, rather than by describing the procedures to be used to accomplish a task. Prolog makes no distinction between the program and data or between data retrieval and computation. It uses formal principles to resolve multiple logical consequences implied by **If-Then** rules or "Horn clauses" in a knowledge base. The classic text on PROLOG is Clocksin and Mellish (1984).[3]

Expert system shells. While many of the early expert systems were developed using languages such as LISP and PROLOG, today most expert systems are developed with the help of programs called "expert system shells." An expert system shell is a program specifically designed for developing expert systems. It consists of three of the four components of expert systems—an inference engine, a knowledge-acquisition interface, and a user interface. All that is lacking is the knowledge base (see Figure 1.1). Using these three components, which have been coded in computer language by a programmer, a social scientist can develop a complete expert system by creating a knowledge base.

Artificial Knowledge (AI) languages and expert system shells are available for the complete spectrum of computers, including AI workstations, mainframes, MS-DOS or UNIX personal computers, Macintoshes, and so on. Popular expert system shells, plus implementations of LISP, PROLOG, and other AI languages for microcomputers, are summarized in the **Appendix.** We will emphasize implementations for widely available MS-DOS and Macintosh computers.

Architecture of Expert Systems

Expert systems typically have four components as illustrated in Figure 1.1 (Brent and Anderson, 1990).

- The **knowledge base** consists of specific knowledge about some substantive domain. A knowledge base differs from a database in that much knowledge in

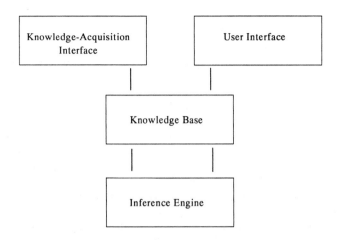

Figure 1.1. The Architecture of Expert Systems

the knowledge base is represented only implicitly. Most of the knowledge is inferred from explicit statements in the knowledge base in conjunction with inferences made by the inference engine. This makes knowledge bases more efficient in data storage than data bases and gives them additional power.

• The **inference engine** uses general rules of inference to reason from explicit knowledge in the knowledge base and to infer additional conclusions, which may not be explicitly stated but can be inferred from other knowledge in the knowledge base. Inference engines are not limited to just mathematical reasoning, or to formal reasoning, but can accommodate both. Many important contemporary problems that are often handled by experts have no formal mathematical solution. They require complex symbolic representations of knowledge, description and integration of knowledge from many levels of abstraction, the ability to handle inconsistent data, and many other capabilities beyond formal mathematics or traditional computer algorithms (Hayes-Roth et al., 1983). Traditional computer algorithms are adequate as long as knowledge is firm, fixed, and formalized, but when knowledge is "subjective, ill-codified, and partly judgmental" (Buchanan, et al., 1983), or when it consists of "heuristic rules of thumb, inconsistent advice, inexact judgmental criteria" (Lenat et al., 1983), then the inference engine of an expert system offers better decision-making capabilities than do traditional computer algorithms.

• The **knowledge-acquisition interface** assists experts in expressing knowledge in a form suitable for incorporation into a knowledge base. Some features commonly provided to assist with knowledge acquisition are traces (lists of rules in the order in which they were "fired," or executed), probes (commands to find and edit specific rules, facts, and so on), and bookkeeping functions and indices (ways to keep track of various features of the knowledge base such as variables and rules). Some expert system shells monitor data entry, checking the syntactic validity of rules. Others provide case facilities — permitting a file of test cases to be stored and automatically evaluated after the program is revised. In addition, many features of the user interfaces, such as on-screen help and explanations, are also of benefit to the developer of expert systems and are often a part of the knowledge-acquisition interface.

- The **user interface** assists users in "consulting" the expert system, prompting them for information required to solve their problem, displaying the program's conclusions, and explaining its reasoning. Generally, these interfaces attempt to provide the user with most of the capabilities they would have if they were interacting with a human expert. Most expert systems, when asked "why" they are asking a question, can explain by displaying explanatory text provided by the author or by showing the user which rule or rules require that information (see BECAUSE in Table 1.1). Many expert systems can also show "how" a value was obtained. Most have some form of on-line context-sensitive help. Most permit users to request definitions of unfamiliar terms. Many can trace the program's reasoning by displaying the sequence of steps it followed in reaching a conclusion. Many permit sensitivity analyses and simulations through a what-if analysis to see how the expert system's conclusions would differ if one or more variables had different values. Some programs display this information graphically, while others use text displays.

Strengths and Weaknesses of Expert Systems

The structure of expert systems offers several advantages over traditional computer programs. By separating the components, expert systems make it possible for different people to develop different parts; the results can be combined to form a workable program. Expert systems permit domain experts having only modest programming skills to develop workable expert programs by simply constructing their own knowledge base that can work with these other components. Thus, knowledgeable persons can create their own systems with little direct programmer involvement.

Because the knowledge base containing domain-specific knowledge is separated from the general reasoning principles embodied in the inference engine, expert systems make it possible to represent knowledge about the domain in a manner that is similar to that used by human experts. This property makes development much easier than converting the knowledge into computer code, and the expert can concentrate on improving the knowledge base and representing knowledge accurately, rather than being distracted by complex and difficult computer programming tasks. In addition, others will find it easier to understand, assess, validate, and maintain the system if its logic is expressed in a more natural language form.

The modularity of the expert system also makes possible operating on same knowledge base with different inference engines. For example, one can test how different theories interpret the same set of facts.

The reliance of expert systems on symbolic reasoning as opposed to purely mathematical reasoning permits them to be applied to problems that were not amenable to traditional numeric programming solutions, thus greatly expanding the scope of applications of computers in the social sciences.

Expert systems often represent knowledge about relatively complex phenomena. For that reason, they may be relatively large, containing hundreds or even thousands of rules or frames. Some form of systematic validation of expert systems is an important requirement. This validation is particularly important, given the informal and even problematic character of much expert system knowledge.

On the bright side, however, expert systems are inherently cumulative. The knowledge system developed by one expert can become the base upon which another expert builds an even more powerful system. Furthermore, once the knowledge is represented correctly and has been validated, the expert system will not forget it or overlook it in the future. The cumulative and lasting character of expert systems is in stark contrast to the knowledge of human experts who age, forget, and may retire or move away. This same argument could be made for using expert systems in the sciences to preserve and sustain the scientific knowledge base across successive generations of scientists.

Analogies. Another way to understand the strengths and limitations of expert systems better is by comparing them to more familiar objects. There are several important ways in which expert systems differ from human experts, manuals, and the numeric algorithms of traditional computer programs.

Just as manuals present the user with considerable information, so do expert systems. Unlike manuals, however, expert systems can tailor their advice to fit the problem of the particular user. With a book, readers may never be quite sure whether or not they have overlooked something important or misunderstood the advice.

Like human experts, expert systems are able to ask users a series of questions, and then, based on those answers, recommend specific actions to be taken, personalized to fit the needs of that person. However, unlike human experts, expert systems are not likely to overlook something, to have a bad day, or to get angry, hostile, or bored.

Expert systems resemble traditional numeric algorithms in that they can systematically address a specific problem and provide a written report to the user. However, unlike numerical algorithms, expert systems do not force every problem into a strict mathematical mold. Expert systems can be applied to a much broader range of problems than numeric algorithms, including qualitative problems that are clearly inappropriate for mathematical solutions. However, because they may use heuristic and unproven strategies, expert systems may produce solutions that have less assurance that they are correct than more formal mathematical algorithms.

Thus we see that expert systems greatly extend the scope of activities that can be successfully computerized, something especially important for the social sciences, where the limitations of formal mathematical approaches have long been noted (Brent, 1986).

Representing and Reasoning About Knowledge

A central problem in expert systems research is the representation problem. Before expert systems can reason symbolically about knowledge, it is necessary to represent knowledge within the computer in such a way that information can be stored and retrieved efficiently, that the knowledge is "faithful" to the phenomenon, and that the computer can "understand" the phenomenon — by manipulating the information in substantively meaningful ways. A text description of knowledge entered by a word processor, for example, may faithfully represent the phenomenon, but to the computer it is merely text rather than knowledge. The computer has no "understanding" of that knowledge and cannot manipulate it in meaningful ways. Mathematical models, on the other hand, can usually be understood and manipulated by the computer but sometimes oversimplify and therefore are unfaithful to the phenomena they are trying to model.

In expert systems, there will usually be linear strings that can be understood from different perspectives. Anderson's (1983: 45) theory of cognition includes three representational types, of which one is a *temporal string,* which encodes the order of a particular set of items. The order in which rules "fire" or are executed in an expert system is an example of this type. A second representation is a *spatial image,* including spatial configurations. These images may sometimes be discoverable for use in expert systems by multidimensional scaling of the paradigmatic representation of all possible combinations of facts or sets of rules. Where these can be displayed in a few dimensions, the underlying causal structure can be revealed, as illustrated in Figure 5.5 for prenatal care (chapter 5). The third representation is *rules* that contain the *meaning of a domain.*[4] Expert systems solve the representation problem in different ways. Most expert systems programs today use *rules* for representing knowledge. *Frames* or *logical expressions* are less commonly employed. *Spatial images* in the form of photographs, drawings, or videos are useful in any of those three. *Strings* are commonly manipulated by AI languages and some shells.

Rule-based systems. Rule-based systems represent knowledge as a series of production rules — statements of the form "**If** x **Then** y" (Waterman and Hayes-Roth, 1978) containing certain antecedent conditions which, when fulfilled, "trigger" or "fire" the rule asserting the consequent to be true. An example rule is as follows:

Example Rule: Milton's (1986) formula for computing sample size for multiple regression or path analysis

IF:
    (1)   Statistical analysis planned is multivariate
and (2)   Multivariate analysis planned is multiple regression, path analysis, structural equation modeling, or LISREL
and (3)   The procedure to be used for computing sample size for multiple regression is Milton's procedure based on the overall r-square and the minimal change in r-square to be considered significant
and (4)   [SHOW_MRM] <>0
and (5)   [MILTREGTITLE]<>'14S9F'
and (6)   [ALPHA100]<>0
and (7)   [TALPHA100]<>0

THEN
    (1)   [SAMSIZMILT] IS GIVEN THE VALUE
          ([K] + 1 + ([TALPHA100]*[TALPHA100])*
          (1-[RSQUARE]/[PARTCOR])
and (2)   The lower limit on sample size has been determined —
          Probability= 99/100
and (3)   Milton's procedure for determining sample size for multiple regression and path analysis has fired

Where
[K] is the number of independent terms in the equation
[TALPHA100] is the value of the t-distribution for this significance level
[RSQUARE] is the proportion variance accounted for by all variables
[PARTCOR] is the partial correlation expected for last variable

NOTE: Milton's formula for computing sample size for multiple regression or path analysis

REFERENCE: Milton, S. (1986) "A Sample Size Formula for Multiple Regression Studies." Public Opinion Quarterly, 50: 112-118.

In this rule, if every antecedent condition in the "**If**" portion of the rule is true, then the expert system will conclude that the consequent conditions in the "**Then**" part are also true. This form of reasoning is called *modus ponens* and takes the general form

If A Then B
A is true
Therefore B is true

Expert systems use reasoning of this sort to derive new "facts," which then become part of the knowledge base. However, it is not possible for all implications to be drawn from this kind of reasoning. For example, consider the following line of reasoning:

If A Then B
Not B
Therefore Not A.

This rule of logic, called *modus tollens* is not implemented in many expert systems. Hence, these expert systems would not be able to conclude that A is not true under such circumstances unless the developer defines additional variables "not B" and "not A," a simple work-around.

Each rule has one or more antecedent conditions (those in the **If** clause) and one or more subsequent conditions (those in the **Then** clause). Rules can vary in complexity, having a single antecedent condition or many antecedent conditions linked by Boolean operators such as "and," "or," "less than," "greater than," and so on. There may also be one or several consequences.

A rule, such as **If X Then Y**" can be represented graphically as a directed path connecting the antecedent to the consequent

By making the antecedents of some rules the consequences of others, these independent rules can be linked in a network of interrelated rules to form an integrated knowledge system such as that diagrammed below.

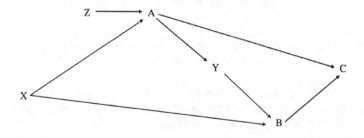

This diagram is equivalent to the following set of rules:

1) **If Z**
   Then A is true
2) **If A**
   Then Y or C is true ["**Then Y** *and* **C**" would be a different
      conclusion.]
3) **If Y**
   Then B is true
4) **If X**
   Then A or B is true
5) **If B**
   Then C is true

Together, these rules may represent complex systems of knowledge. Many existing rule-based programs contain hundreds of rules. Complex problems can be broken down into simpler components each of which when solved contributes to the solution of the larger problem. **If-Then** rules may be constructed to represent a wide variety of knowledge types, including formulae, statements about causality, logical classifications, logical statements, principles, and even informal rules of thumb (Brent, 1986).

In addition to making inferences from known facts and the knowledge in the knowledge base, inference engines also use various control strategies. In rule-based systems the inference engine interprets the rules in the knowledge base, traces their antecedents to determine what facts need to be known to fire each rule, decides in what order to examine various rules, and asks questions of the user where necessary in order to determine information needed to fire rules. A common control strategy is **backward-chaining** (or goal-driven reasoning), which begins with a goal or objective, then identifies rules that have that goal as a consequence. It then looks at the antecedents of those rules to determine if their values are known. If not, it identifies rules for which those are consequences, looks for antecedents to those rules, and continues this backward-chaining process until it finds antecedents having no rules for deducing them. Then it asks the user for the values of those antecedents.

Another strategy — often called **forward-chaining**, data-driven, or antecedent-driven control structure (Waterman and Hayes-Roth, 1978) — begins with data input by the user and scans the rules to find those whose antecedent conditions are fulfilled by the data. It then fires those rules and deduces their consequences. The consequences are added to the knowledge base and the rules are reexamined to see what new rules may now be fired. This process is repeated with rules firing whenever possible, and new information is added to the knowledge base until all rules have been fired that can be fired.

In the example above, in order to illustrate the **backward-chaining** approach, let us make C the goal. If A or B were true, we could conclude that C was true. The expert system would check to see whether it knew if B (then A) was true, since if either were true, it could conclude that C was true. This goal-oriented approach is distinctive of backward-chaining procedures. In order to know that A or B was true, the system would try to determine that if X or Y was true, B would be true, and would next try to determine the truth value of X and Y. If it could be concluded that X was true, then B is true; if B is true, then C is true, and the system would stop, having arrived at a solution by backward-chaining.[5] If the **forward-chaining** strategy were employed, the program would first determine whether Z, then X were true; if, say, Z were true, the program would know that A was true, and would be able to conclude C true. In this simple example, there is little reason to choose either forward- or backward-chaining methods over the other, but there are circumstances in which one would be preferable to the other. Forward-chaining expert systems have the advantage of being much faster than backward-chaining ones. On the other hand, in backward-chaining systems the answer to a single question may rule out a conclusion, whereas forward-chaining systems usually require that more questions be asked. If these are primarily answered by the user, rather than, say, a data base, the system may appear clumsy. Where there are many possible goals, and only a relatively small number of antecedents, a forward-chaining system will perform better. However, since forward-chaining expert systems tend to ask too many questions, the user may not find them as "intelligent" as backward-chainers. Backward-chaining expert systems tend to perform more like a human would, by first ruling out "obviously" incorrect conclusions before starting to work back up the antecedents which, if true, would verify a particular conclusion as acceptable.

Any rule-based system can be represented as either a forward- or a backward-chaining model. Beginning developers tend to prefer forward-chaining because it is more like a decision tree or a taxonomy. Generally, backward-chainers are preferred by experienced developers and users because of their ability to mimic human reasoning. Some shells permit a mixture of forward- and backward-chaining subcomponents of the system. Most permit a fixed series of questions to be asked before beginning a backward-chaining session.

Obviously, where all items of a questionnaire or protocol must be obtained in any case, a forward-chaining expert system is preferred due to its speed. The more interactive, "human-like" performance of a backward-chaining expert system is probably more generally useful. Some shells, such as EXSYS,[6] have as an option an intermediate hybrid form, which proceeds in the order of rules, but obtains information needed for a particular rule by backward-chaining.

Logic-based systems. PROLOG programs produce logic-based systems. In logic-based systems knowledge is often represented in the form of assertions. The statement

relation (a,b)

asserts that "a" has some "relation" with "b." For example,

is_a(sam,physician)

asserts that Sam is a physician.

Objects may be constants (conventionally beginning with lowercase letters) or variables (which begin with uppercase letters). For example,

is_a(X,physician)

asserts that "X" is a physician, where X is a variable which might be assigned or "instantiated" as "Sam," "Mary," or some other person.

If-Then rules may be represented in PROLOG as follows:

y :- x

which is read, "y if x" or "y is true if x is true." For example, the following

grandfather_of(sam,charles) :-
 father_of(bill,charles),
 father_of(sam,bill).

asserts Sam is the grandfather of Charles if Bill is the father of Charles and Sam is the father of Bill.

Resolution. Logical systems such as those written in PROLOG use a method of inference called "resolution," which is a strategy for determining whether a particular fact is valid, given all the other knowledge in the knowledge base (see Clocksin and Mellish, 1984). For example, an expert system capable of resolution having the following knowledge within its knowledge base

Martha is the mother of John
Sam is the father of John
Martha is the mother of Susan
William is the father of Susan

is able to correctly answer the following questions:

Question	Answer
Is Martha the mother of John?	*[YES]*
Is Sam the father of Susan?	*[NO]*
Who is Susan's father?	*[WILLIAM]*

Frame-based systems. Frames (Minsky, 1975) are data structures which describe stereotypical situations. Each frame consists of several slots each of which represents a specific type of information. Slots are filled by fillers, which may be specific information, a default value, nothing, or a pointer to another frame. For example, in Figure 1.2, which illustrates an episode in the expert system ERVING, the *"Joe"* frame describing the person, Joe, contains several slots *(Personal Goals, Personal Characteristics, Roles, Generalizations, and Specializations)*. Some slots are filled with specific information (e.g., the *Personal Characteristics* of Joe are *male* and *21*), others are blank (e.g., Joe's *Personal Goals* are unknown and are left blank), others are filled in with default information, which is presumed to be true in the absence of explicit information to the contrary (e.g., the *General Goals* for actors are presumed to include "present idealized performance" — a hypothesis of Erving Goffman's dramaturgical perspective (1959) — unless otherwise indicated), while others are filled with pointers to other frames (e.g., the *Frontstage Setting* slot for the *Waiter* frame points to the dining room; and the *Generalizations* slot for the *Waiter* frame points to a frame describing the general concept of role in more detail), permitting several frames to be linked to one another to represent complex information.

Inheritance and frame-based reasoning. Some of the slots in Figure 1.2 have special significance. The *Generalizations* and *Specializations* slots permit frames to be linked together in a hierarchy from most general to most specific. This permits great economies of representation because properties of more general frames can be inherited by the more specific equivalents and need not be respecified again. For example, the *Waiter* frame can inherit general properties of roles from the *Role* frame, for which it is a special case. Frames can also be used to represent both **declarative**, or static knowledge (e.g., facts such as who, what, where, and so on) and **procedural** knowledge (e.g., directions such as "If this is true, then do that"). Procedural knowledge is often represented by production rules where procedures are attached to specific slots or to entire frames (see Aikens, 1983). The latter strategy is used here and is illustrated in Figure 1.2 where, for example, the *Personal Characteristics* slot for the *Joe* frame has a procedural attachment which, when sex is unknown, attempts to infer sex from the name.

Using the knowledge as represented in Figure 1.2, the ERVING program is capable of reasoning about the kinds of interaction that do and do not occur in such settings. For example, the program can answer the question "Why did Joe not sample the pudding with his finger in the dining room?" by the following train of logic. First, it notes that Joe is in the dining room. Using additional reasoning not displayed in Figure 1.2, it determines that the dining room is a "frontstage" setting for Joe, playing the role of waiter. Then it scans the personal goals of Joe, the role-specific expectations for waiter, and even general goals of actors, to eventually find the general goal of "presenting an idealized performance." Finally, it establishes that this goal is inconsistent with the action "sampling the pudding" in that frontstage setting. From this reasoning process it generates an explanation for why this act does or does not occur, which reflects its reasoning in much the same way a human expert might explain his or her own reasoning.

Each knowledge representation strategy has advantages and disadvantages and may be more or less appropriate for specific applications. Buchanan (1985), for example, suggests rules have the advantage of a simple syntax, which makes them both more flexible than some other representations and easier to understand. Frames have greater expressive power because it is easy to set up slots for new properties, relations, and specialized procedures "on-the-fly." Logic systems, compiled AI

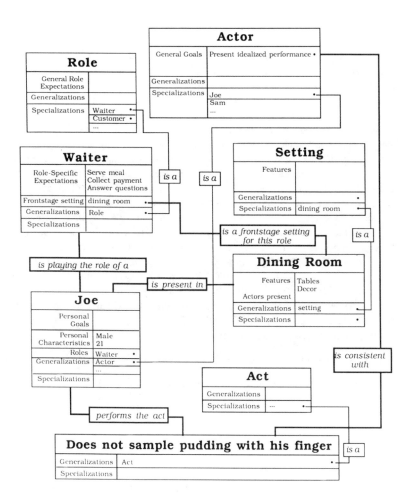

Figure 1.2. An Episode in the Expert System ERVING

languages, are primarily *nonprocedural languages* permitting facts to be asserted independent of their use and can use their built-in resolution algorithm to assure that the knowledge base is logically consistent.

Any particular expert system may use one or more of these representation and reasoning strategies. For example, an expert system written in PROLOG or Knowledge-Pro could represent both rules and frames within the language and use logic as well.

Confidence factors and uncertainty. Many social science problems require reasoning under uncertainty. Rule-based systems can handle uncertainty by specifying what are called confidence factors. Rules that employ devices for specifying certainty are usually termed **heuristics.** Two major issues are (1) estimation of "confidence" factors and (2) their combination. In some instances, confidence factors may be considered to be equivalent to probabilities, and their combination might proceed in a classical manner. However, more often in expert system development, they involve subjective estimates. Ng and Abramson (1990) have a useful discussion of confidence factors. Bayesian methods are sometimes employed, although other methods are common. Fuzzy logic (see Negoita, 1985) is another natural metaphor that requires a few assumptions as to the properties of the confidence factors. Expert system shells are somewhat idiosyncratic in their selection of methods to manipulate confidence factors and often use definition methods depending on their location within the rule. Most programs permit the user to specify confidence factors, or certainty values, and some, such as VP-EXPERT, permit the user to enter them during consultation. These numbers typically range from 1 to 100 (although other systems are used), and are treated *as if* they were probabilities of some sort. These certainty values are then combined in one of a number of ways to estimate the certainty value for the premise, conclusion, and/or the strength of the entire rule.

For example, consider the following rule:

If A and B **Then** C

We might assign the following certainty values: A = .8 and B = .1

Then the certainty factor for the strength of the rule might be computed from these values in a number of ways, such as:

1) dependent certainties are often combined as the product of individual certainties:

CFA $*$ CFB (.8) $*$ (.1) = .08

2) "independent" certainties are often combined as

$[1 - (1 - CFA) * (1 - CFB)]$:

$1 - (1 - .8) * (1 - .1) = .98$

3) dependent certainties may be combined by taking the lowest value, min (PA, PB):

min (.8, .1) = .1 [fuzzy *and*]

4) independent certainties may be combined by taking the highest value,
max (PA, PB):
max (.8, .1) = .8 [fuzzy *or*)

The first two of these methods are available in the EXSYS and several other shells. Unfortunately, the product of two or more uncertainties (case 1 above) is mislabeled *independent* both in the manual and in the program. The second independent method is mislabeled *dependent* in EXSYS. Moreover, this independent formula does not correspond to the classical method of combining estimates of individual events ([P(A) * P(B/A)] of probability theory. Instead, formula 2 above has the effect of *adding* to a confidence factor any new information as the product of the uncertainty remaining times the new uncertainty. The implications of applying fuzzy set theory to expert systems have been extensively discussed by Negoita (1985). Fuzzy *and* or *or* is used in many expert system shells, such as VP EXPERT and the Intelligent Developer. The Intelligent Developer is eclectic in using the accretion method for *or* and fuzzy combination for *and* (and other operators, see p. 53 in the Version 1.0 manual). Bayesian combination may seem natural where there are subjective prior confidence estimates that are to be combined with objective ones.

To recapitulate, we have introduced in this chapter the essential features of expert systems and their representations and manipulations of knowledge. In the following chapters, we first review kinds of expert system applications in the social sciences, then trace the development of an expert system in some detail.

2. APPLICATIONS OF EXPERT SYSTEMS IN THE SOCIAL SCIENCES

In this chapter we identify a wide range of expert systems in the social sciences. There are now quite a number of social science expert systems, and they have been applied to virtually every aspect of the research process. The objectives of this chapter are to convey the broad scope of expert systems, to identify existing expert systems that may be of interest to particular readers, and to stimulate readers to think of ways expert systems might be applied to their own areas of interest. (Readers already familiar with the range of expert systems may wish to skip this chapter to focus first on issues of knowledge acquisition, pragmatic strategies for developing expert systems, and validating expert systems in Chapters 3, 4, and 5.)

In Figure 2.1 is a summary of expert systems applications in the social sciences, organized by the steps in the research process that they address. The applications described in this chapter are predominantly normative. Many guide the researcher, suggesting research strategies, critiquing research plans, and encouraging thoroughness and consistency in investigation. We also describe various applications of expert systems as research models.

Theorizing
  Assessing whether a theory is well-formed (Sylvan and Glassner 1985)
  Comparing theories
  Explicating underlying policies (Brent et al. 1986)
  Simulations
  Cognitive Modeling (Furbee 1989, Benfer 1989, Read and Behrens 1989)
Defining the Research Problem
  Defining the research problem . . . PROBDEF (Brent 1990)
Designing the Research
  Determining a sampling strategy . . . EX-SAMPLE+ (Brent et al. 1988, 1989b)
  Selecting appropriate data collection procedures . . . DATA COLLECTION SELECTION
        (Brent 1989f)
  Experimental design . . . EXPERIMENTAL DESIGN, DESIGNER RESEARCH
        (Brent and Miriellei 1989)
  Selection of appropriate statistics . . . STATISTICAL NAVIGATOR (Brent 1988a, 1988b)
  Questionnaire construction . . . MEASUREMENT & SCALING STRATEGIST
        (Brent 1989e)
Data Collection
  Computer-assisted coding of qualitative data . . . SKI (Carley 1988)
  Collection of qualitative data . . . QUALOG (Shelly and Sibert 1986)
  Eliciting sequential or hierarchical data . . . ETHNO (Heise and Lewis 1988)
Data Analysis
  Automatic analysis of data sets . . . RX (Blum 1984)
  AI search procedures to find causal models (Glymour et al. 1987)
  Induction of rules from cases (Garson 1987; Brent et al. 1986)
  Analysis of qualitative data . . . QUALOG (Shelly and Sibert 1986)
Teaching
  Intelligent computer-assisted instruction (ICAI) . . . ERVING (Brent et al. 1989a)
  Models of student behavior ERVING (Brent et al. 1989a)
  Critiquing (Clancy 1987); EX-SAMPLE+ (Brent et al. 1989b)
Applications, Disseminating Research Findings
  Government
  Social services
  Education
  Psychology and psychiatry
  Extension

Figure 2.1. Applications of Expert Systems to Steps in the Research Process

Applications of Expert Systems to Theorizing

Expert systems and artificial intelligence techniques have been used in several ways to assist in developing social science theories. They have been used to model or simulate social phenomena and to examine the logical consistency of a theory.

Examine the logical consistency of a theory. Sylvan and Glassner (1985) illustrate an entirely different use of artificial intelligence techniques in theory development. They use logic programming to examine an existing theory by translating many of the theoretical assertions in Simmel's work (1955) into statements in an artificial intelligence programming language, LOGLISP. LOGLISP, which stands for logic and LISP, permits programs to be written that can both make deductions and explain them in a manner not possible in many other kinds of programming languages. In this work, Sylvan and Glassner (1985) translate 107 passages from Simmel into 223 formalized statements. Sylvan and Glassner illustrate this process of translation with the following passage from Simmel:

> We confront the stranger, with whom we share neither characteristics nor broader interests, objectively; we hold our personalities in reserve; and thus a particular difference does not involve us in our totalities. On the other hand, we meet the person who is very different from us only on certain points within a particular context or within a coincidence of particular interests, and hence the spread of the conflict is limited to those points only. The more we have in common with another *as whole persons,* however, the more easily will our totality be involved in every single relation to him (Simmel, 1955: 44).

This passage is translated into four separate statements as in the Table 2.1 below:

TABLE 2.1 Simmel's Hypotheses Translated into LOGLISP

(H16a1 (IR Objective) <– (IA Strangers) (GA Big))
(H16a2 (IR Objective) <– (IA Strangers) (GA Small))

(H16b1 (IR Conflict) <– (Direct (IA Different)) (IA Similar) (GA Big))
(H16b2 (IR Conflict) <– (Direct (IA Different)) (IA Similar) (GA Small))

where
H16__ refers to the number of hypotheses,
IR is a relation among individuals (here, either conflict or objective),
IA are individual attributes (here, different or strangers),
GA are group attributes (here, either big or small)

H16a1 and H16a2 assert that "in either big or small groups, individuals who are strangers will relate to each other objectively." H16b1 and H16b2 mean "in either big or small groups, individuals who are strangers will relate to each other objectively." H16b1 and H16b2 mean "in either big or small groups, conflict between individuals is restricted to their immediate points of difference and enhanced insofar as they are similar."

Sylvan and Glassner then use LOGLISP to determine whether those theoretical assertions lead logically to informative assertions, whether the theory is illogical and internally contradictory, and whether those assertions permit the computer to deduce a central tenet of Simmel's work, the conflict-cohesion hypothesis. They found the resulting program capable of generating informative assertions, and they found little evidence of illogic in the assertions themselves. However, although they were able to deduce from these assertions specific versions of the conflict-cohesion hypothesis, they were unable to deduce the most general form of this assertion. Their work illustrates one application of AI to sociological theorizing by using a logically rigorous AI language to check the logical consistency and the logical connectedness of a sociological theory. Read and Behrens (1989) recast a difficult axiomatic formalism of Bisayan terms of address (Geoghegan, 1971) into production rules. This anthropological expert system, BATES, bridged the gap between abstract formalism and verbal reasoning, in a model both more accessible as well as more parsimonious. Blank (1989) uses this same general approach to assess the work of Moore (1966).

Modeling: Use of an AI Program as the Theory Itself

Several authors have used relatively straightforward rule-based expert systems to model social phenomena. In political science, this approach has been used to model energy policy in Japan (Bobrow et al., 1986), general foreign policy (Hudson, 1987; Schrodt, 1989), Jimmy Carter's political views (Lane, 1986), involvement in the Vietnam War (Majeski, 1987), Soviet policy (Kaw, 1986), and Chinese foreign policy (Tanaka, 1984).

Banerjee (1986) used logic programming to create an artificial intelligence program representing social structures as preferences and judgments of social causality by participants in a particular historical situation. He argued that social structures endure only when the preferences and judgments of participants prompt them to act in ways that reinforce the preferences and judgments of other participants. When actions of each set of participants reinforced the preferences and judgments of others, that particular social structure tended to reproduce itself and to be stable over time. He employed this PROLOG program to represent two different specific historical circumstances using this model — Skocpol's (1979) analysis of China's sociopolitical structure of the 1930s, and O'Donnell's (1973) analysis of the bureaucratic authoritarian structure in the Latin America of the 1960s. Banerjee argued that both of these social structures tend to be self-reproducing. Banerjee's work is an example of the use of artificial intelligence programming strategies where the AI program becomes the theory itself. It permits the developer to simulate some social situation and examine the consequences of potential acts.

Several authors have noted the striking similarity between expert systems and simulations (O'Keefe, 1986). An active literature is developing on the use of AI in simulation. The Society for Computer Simulation International, for example, has published a series of proceedings on the topic (Webster, 1989). In the social sciences, there are several examples of this approach. Garson (1989) and Schrodt (1989) each discuss the role of expert systems for simulation in political science. Cimbala (1987) provides several examples.

Simulating Actual Historical Events
(Simulating a Theory with an Expert System)

Thorsan and Sylvan (1982) used a rule-based production system to simulate John F. Kennedy's decisions during the Cuban Missile Crisis. They represented Kennedy's decision processes as **If . . . Then** rules in a computer program and first ran the program with events and circumstances like those that actually happened in the Cuban Missile Crisis. The program produced simulated responses of Kennedy much like those that we know occurred. They then ran the program several other times with different sets of events ("counterfactuals"), which did not actually occur, to explore how Kennedy might have reacted in varying circumstances. Thus they used this artificial-intelligence-based program to create a simulation of an actual historical series of events and then used it to simulate other hypothetical chains of events.

The representation of sociological theories using artificial intelligence techniques has posed a number of problems, including how to adequately represent concepts such as norms, values, and beliefs that vary from one individual to the next; the meaning of utterances; attempts at deception; and so on (Allen and Perrault, 1980).

Brent (1986) shows how a wide range of theoretical assertions can be easily translated from English into logical assertions in PROLOG (see Table 2.2). He goes on to illustrate how PROLOG can represent social science concepts such as norms, levels of aggregation, contextual effects and emergent properties, attitudes, values, and beliefs.

Brent et al. (1989a) combine logic programming, frames, and procedural rules to elaborate and extend an existing sociological theory into an expert system, ERVING, that uses these techniques to teach undergraduate students to reason about phenomena from the dramaturgical perspective. Unlike Sylvan and Glassner (1985), who try to translate specific theoretical assertions faithfully from Simmel's work into computer language equivalents, Brent et al. attempt to test the logical assertions made by Goffman using PROLOG. They employ the computer to elaborate that sociological theory. For them, the dramaturgical perspective forms a basis for developing specific assertions that may go beyond the original theory in specificity and complexity (see also Read and Behrens, 1989, for an anthropological example).

Expert Systems for Designing and Conducting Research

Another active area of applications of expert systems is in the design and conduct of social science research. A wide range of programs are available for designing various aspects of research projects. These include a number of programs to determine

TABLE 2.2 Example Translations from English into PROLOG (Excerpted from Brent 1986)

ENGLISH	PROLOG
performance refer(s) to all the activity of an individual which occurs during a period marked by his continuous presence before a particular set of observers and which has some influence on the observers. . . .	is_a (X, performance) if is_a(X, activity) and occurs_during(X,Period) and marked_by(Period and contin_pres_of_(Obsvs)) and influences(X,Obsvs).
First, there is the "setting involving furniture, decor, physical layout, and other background items which supply the scenery and stage props. . . .	part_of(furniture,setting). part_of(decor,setting). part_of(phys_layout,setting). part_of(stage_props,setting).
"front" that part of the individual's performance which regularly functions in a general and fixed fashion to define the situation for those who observe. . . .	is_a(X,front) if part_of(X,individs_perform) and defines_sitn_for(X,Obsvs).

*In PROLOG, functions are expressed in the form
    relation (A,B)
where this means A has some relation to B. For example,
    is_a(X,Y)
is a function which asserts that X is a Y.

sample size (Goldstein, 1989) and several programs to design experiments (e.g., see EXPERIMENTAL DESIGN™). However, most of these programs use traditional programming techniques rather than artificial intelligence techniques.

Exceptions are the expert systems in Methodologist's Toolchest from the Idea Works. They include EX-SAMPLE+™, a program to conduct a power analysis and determine the appropriate sample size (Brent et al., 1989b); STATISTICAL NAVIGATOR™, a program to help select the appropriate statistic (Brent, 1988a); DESIGNER RESEARCH™, a program to design experiments (Brent and Mirielli, 1989), MEASUREMENT & SCALING STRATEGIST™, a program to construct questionnaires (Brent, 1989e); and DATA COLLECTION SELECTION™, a program to select the appropriate means of data collection (Brent, 1989f).

These programs typically ask a series of questions about your objectives and assumptions, much as a human expert might. Then, based on responses, they recommend a particular analysis or design. They try to emulate the human expert not only in the quality of recommendations but also in the style of interaction permitted (Brent, 1989b, 1989c, 1989d). The approach is illustrated by the STATISTICAL NAVIGATOR™, a program that helps users select the appropriate form of statistical analysis. STATISTICAL NAVIGATOR™ first asks the user a series of questions to identify his or her analysis objectives and the assumptions they are willing to make about the data. In many cases the user may be unable or unwilling to provide an absolute "yes/no" answer, in which case the program lets users specify a confidence level rather than an absolute yes or no answer. This is illustrated by the following example question:

Please input on a scale from 0 (least) to 10 (most) how confident are you these variables are measured at the nominal level:

If the user doesn't understand a question he or she can ask for a clarification. For example, if one enters "?", when queried whether the analysis should use a symmetric measure, the user will view the following clarification.

SYMMETRIC MEASURE?

A symmetric measure is one which does not distinguish independent variables and dependent variables. It will produce the same result when assessing the relationship between a and b and when assessing the relationship between b and a. The Pearson product-moment correlation coefficient is an example of a symmetric measure. The correlation of x and y is the same as that for y and x. The regression coefficient, on the other hand, is an asymmetric measure. The regression of x on y is not necessarily the same as the regression of y on x.

Users can also ask "why" and see a display of the rule or rules that require the information. This feature helps the user understand the reasoning the program is employing during the consultation.

When these programs conclude their reasoning, they provide report containing recommendations. STATISTICAL NAVIGATOR™ gives a detailed report written in an ASCII text file on disk and displayed on the monitor. The user can then take a report, edit it with a word processor, and integrate it into a research proposal or publication. The report begins with a summary of its over-all recommendations (in this case, a rank ordering of the four best statistical analyses for the problem described by the user).

Summary Scores for Four Most Promising Analysis Techniques

Technique	Preference Based On		
	Goals	Assumptions	Audience Receptivity
1) Krippendorff's r	0.970	0.980	0.300
2) intraclass correl, ri	0.970	0.980	0.300
3) Cohen's k	0.970	0.860	0.850
Krippendorff's rbar	0.970	0.730	0.200

ᵇest possible score is 1.0, the worst is 0.

That overview is then followed by a detailed description of each of the recommended analyses including references, common statistical packages which perform that analysis, and a point-by-point consideration of how each technique does or does not fit the problem described. (Below are the detailed comments for one of these analyses.)

Detailed Explanation of Four Preferred Techniques

Cohen's Kappa

Preference Score: 0.967
Assumptions Score: 0.860

Description:

Cohen's kappa (Cohen, 1960) is a measure of agreement between two raters classifying a sample of items into one of k mutually exclusive and exhaustive unordered categories.

Cohen's kappa is adjusted for chance agreement so that it equals zero when observed agreement equals chance agreement, negative when observed agreement is less than that expected by chance alone, and equal to 1.0 when there is perfect agreement.

Significance Tests:

For significance tests of kappa, see Fleiss, Cohen, and Everitt (1969); Reynolds (1977).

References:

Cohen (1960, 1968); Reynolds (1977); Fleiss (1981);
Fleiss, Cohen, and Everitt (1969)

Statistical Packages:

OSIRIS TABLES, BMDP P4F

Objectives and Assumptions:

Analysis goals:	Ideal	Reported
measure agreement or reliability	10	10
assess consistency within multi-item scale	0	0
penalize for marginals which disagree	0	1

Assumptions	Ideal	Reported
assess agreement or reliability among multiple vars	0	0
assess agreement or reliability among two variables	10	10
variables measured at nominal level	10	3
variables measured in discrete categories	10	10
variables have multiple categories	10	10

Expert Systems and Data Collection

Carley (1988) developed an expert system to assist with the coding of qualitative data. She employed a two-stage computer-assisted procedure in which a novice coder would use one computer program (CODEF) to code verbal data initially, then those data would be further processed, using an expert system (SKI). The expert system is based on social knowledge and contains a cognitive model of how an expert researcher uses that knowledge to make coding decisions. Carley reports that this procedure reduces the time required to train the novice coder and increases reliability of data. Other researchers employ artificial intelligence techniques to collect data using computers or describe procedures that could be implemented using such techniques. Franzosi (1989), for example, describes a way of coding data from textual sources based on the linguistic concept of a semantic text grammar that could be implemented using AI techniques. Heise and Lewis's (1988) ETHNO is a computer program that can be used as a data elicitation device to assist in data collection. Shelly and Sibert (1986) describe QUALOG, a set of mainframe computer programs using LOGLISP to assist with the collection and analysis of qualitative data.

There are also implications for data collection when expert systems are used in the field to represent a tentative theory and provide a stimulus to respondents to test the validity of that theory. Expert systems have been used in this way in anthropology to test music grammars (Kippen, 1988) and agricultural models (Furbee, 1989; Benfer and Furbee, 1989).

Data Analysis

Programs that induce rules or theories from data may be viewed as another kind of data analysis program. It is easy to imagine (though much harder to implement) programs that could help users with all aspects of data analysis, from selecting the appropriate statistics, to helping the user manage data, to specifying the details of the analysis, to helping interpret the results. An edited volume of papers from a workshop on expert systems in statistics includes several papers suggesting ways in which expert systems can be applied to statistical analysis (Haux, 1986).

Induction of a theory from data. Brent et al. (1986), Garson (1987), Schrodt (1989), Benfer and Furbee (1989b), and Furbee (1989) illustrate application of expert systems and artificial intelligence techniques to the development of theories. Each uses an inductive expert system to generate initial theoretical propositions from data that can be refined and elaborated. These inductive expert systems create decision-tree-like rules for predicting a dependent variable from a small set of independent variables. Schrodt (1989: 120) reports that 38 variables were reduced to five, which were able to predict 95% to 100% of the cases in the full-sample tests; however, only 50% to 60% were correctly predicted in split-sample tests. The results of the inductive expert system are often compared with the results of traditional regression modeling procedures applied to the same data. While these papers are not all unqualified in endorsing this approach, they do illustrate its potential for developing theoretical propositions from data.

Heuristic search for models of empirical data. Glymour et al. (1987) illustrate another application of expert systems and artificial intelligence techniques to developing theories, causal models. TETRAD uses heuristic search techniques from artificial intelligence to look for alternative causal models to account for particular data sets. This program can be used by a researcher to help identify promising causal models based on particular data sets; these models can be compared to those initially hypothesized by the researcher. Although not guaranteed to provide the best solution, these heuristic search procedures greatly narrow the possible combinations and make it possible to search a very complex set of possible solutions for this problem.

Cognitive Modeling

An important application of expert systems in the social sciences is the use of expert systems to help us better understand the way groups of people in particular subcultures think about things or find meaning in their lives. In psychology and anthropology, this approach has been used to understand how the mind works by viewing it as an information processing system (e.g., Posner, 1990; Geoghegan, 1971). In management science, an example of cognitive modeling is policy analysis in which expert systems (or more commonly traditional statistical regression models) are used to examine the decision processes that people use, by estimating the impact of various factors on those decisions (e.g., see Brent et al., 1986).

In anthropology this approach has been used to develop an expert system to account for the classification of soils and the management of crops in a farming community in the highlands of Southern Perú. Farming depends on a system of terrace agriculture, and farmers there have had excellent yields. In other parts of Perú, some of this technology has been lost, so the Lari Project was designed to record this indigenous knowledge toward making it available to other Andean communities.

Furbee (1989) used an expert system to model the ways that Andean farmers classify soils and manage crops (FAI-SOILS (F = "Folk") and FAI-CROPS). Rules for FAI-SOILS were induced using the 1stCLASS shell from a list of terms obtained from five local farmers — the native consultants for the study. Using adaptations of standard ethnoscience techniques (see Werner and Schoepfle, 1987; Furbee, 1989), a model was developed from four of the consultants, each of whom provided features for soil types. Each consultant's set of features was entered separately and weighted equally. The assumption was that there are multiple pathways available to classify a soil type. When the Multiple Pathways model produced from the first four consultants was tested for validity with data from the fifth, all 17 of the soil types from the reserved informant were classified correctly by the pooled expert system. A simpler model was obtained from a single matrix whose entries were the modal values (yes, maybe, or no), of the four (see Tables 2 and 3 in Furbee, 1989). However, three errors were found with the simpler model.

EXTENT OF THE PROBLEM

EX-SAMPLE has determined that the minimum sample size required for 2 of the analyses planned exceed(s) the maximum possible sample size given the available resources for this study.

CAN YOU SWITCH TO A ONE-TAILED TEST?

You chose to do a two-tailed test. If you can use a one-tailed test, sample size can be significantly reduced.

ARE THE PROPORTIONS REALLY SO NEAR .5?

As the proportions near .5 required sample size generally increases. Your estimated proportions are near .5. Are you sure this is the case? If the actual values are farther from .5, the required sample size will be reduced.

CAN YOU INCREASE THE EFFECT SIZE?

The recommended sample size is very sensitive to the part correlation (the proportion of variance to be accounted for by the smallest path to be considered significant). The larger the part correlation, the smaller the necessary sample size. If you could theoretically justify increasing your part correlation to, say .1, you could reduce the sample size requirements for the two sample comparison of proportions.

Figure 2.2. Partial Excerpt from EX-SAMPLE 2.0+ Critique Grantsmanship

Teaching

Computer-assisted instruction is one of the areas where expert systems were first applied (e.g., Sleeman and Brown, 1982). An approach often taken is one called ICAI (Intelligent Computer-Assisted Instruction) in which the expert system includes not only the substantive domain knowledge base, but also a separate knowledge base regarding the student. The latter knowledge base is used during the interaction with students to model their behavior and infer what kinds of help they require.

Some of the social science expert system programs cited earlier are designed for teaching. ERVING is designed exclusively for teaching purposes. Programs in the Methodologist's Toolchest are designed both for teaching and field applications. EX-SAMPLE+™ illustrates the use of a critiquing strategy that was developed in the ICAI literature. This program first assists the researcher in specifying the sample size, then it critiques the plan, offering suggestions for changes that might reduce the required sample size or increase the possible size given constraints on resources. A partial excerpt from an EX-SAMPLE+ critique is provided in Figure 2.2.

Applying and Disseminating Knowledge

Briefly, these are some of the areas in which expert systems are being applied. Expert systems in government is an area receiving considerable attention. There are annual conferences on this topic, and expert systems are being developed to help determine eligibility for government benefits programs (Sear, 1988) and to enforce regulations of various types (e.g., Taft, 1988). Many of these expert systems could also be viewed as expert systems in social services. Other examples of social service oriented expert systems are commercial systems such as HOME-SAFE-HOME (a program that assesses the home environment of elderly persons and recommends ways to make their homes safer, more functional, and more comfortable, R. Brent et al., in revision), EXPERCARE (a program recommending the appropriate level of care in which to place elderly persons), and LOCUS (an expert system recommending the appropriate level of care for mental patients). Another area of application is in education. We have already talked about how expert systems have been used and could be used to develop intelligent computer-assisted instruction. Other expert systems in education have been used to assess educational deficits of particular students (e.g., Hofmeister and Lubke, 1988). Another area is the application of expert systems in clinical psychology and psychiatry (e.g., see Hedlund and Vieweg, 1988). There, expert systems applications range from diagnosing psychotic disorders (Overby, 1987) to assessing sexual dysfunction (Binik et al., 1988) to consultation for emotional crises (Hedlund et al., 1987). There are even commercially available expert systems in this area for diagnosing personality disorders (e.g., DTREE, The Psychiatry Expert, and Decisionbase).

A final area is the application of expert systems in anthropology. AI-FORENS, mentioned in Chapter 1 (Benfer et al., 1990) was also developed to disseminate knowledge, that of forensic anthropologists. AI-FORENS is comprised of a group of related expert systems, each of which models the knowledge used by a forensic expert to determine the age and sex of an individual from the innominate bone of the skeleton. AI-FORENS will make the expertise of these leading scientists available to coroners, to students of forensic anthropology, and to others, as both an application and a teaching tool.

The FAI-SOILS and FAI-CROPS expert systems mentioned above are also examples of applications of expert systems. They model the farming knowledge of successful Peruvian terrace agriculturalists and, as such, had to incorporate the knowledge of several experts since no one person had complete experience with all aspects of all fields in the community. One way to achieve this incorporation of the knowledge of several persons was to create a "modal model," which treated variation as error. A sample from the modal model for the FAI-SOILS expert system is given in Table 2.3. In a second version of FAI-SOILS, which was called a Multiple Pathways model, rules for an expert system to predict the classification of soils were induced with the 1stCLASS shell from a list of terms obtained from local informants, using standard ethnoscience techniques (see Chapter 3).

Another expert system constructed on the folk knowledge of an Andean community is FAI-HEAL, which models the decision-making of residents of the Quechua community of Callalli, also in the Colca Valley of Perú. FAI-HEAL predicts from whom medical treatment will be sought: a household member, a curer, or a practitioner of Western medicine (health paraprofessional, nurse, or physician) for each of several indigenously recognized illnesses (Furbee, 1987; Jackson, 1987). The Callalli resi-

TABLE 2.3 Two Rules from FAI-SOILS

Rule 1		Rule 2	
	If the soil is not salty		If the soil is not salty
and	if soil does not rot roots	and	if soil does not rot roots
and	if the soil is not hard	and	if the soil is not hard
and	if the soil is soft	and	if the soil is soft
and	if the soil is not silty	and	if the soil is not silty
and	if the soil does grow maiz	and	if the soil is not clayey
and	if the soil does not need fertilizer	and	if the soil is weak (thin)
and	if the soil is weak (thin)	and	if the soil is white
and	if the soil is white		
and	if the soil is clayey		then the soil is **akku**
	then the soil is **allin hallp'a**		

dents chose Western medical practitioners for serious cases of "Western" illnesses, for example, for measles. For what were perceived as indigenous illnesses (e.g., ancestor illness), they chose a curer. Household residents, many of whom had sophisticated knowledge of herbal medicine, were usually consulted first and were the sole providers of care for illnesses that were not perceived as life-threatening.

3. KNOWLEDGE ACQUISITION

The acquisition of knowledge from human experts is one of the central problems faced in developing expert systems (Diaper, 1989). The task is by no means trivial. In fact, knowledge acquisition is usually conducted in an ad hoc manner, despite the fact that there has been considerable discussion of the issue in the AI literature (Hoffman, 1987), and even some expert systems designed that attempt to automate the knowledge acquisition process, using various strategies (e.g., Auto-Intelligence, Intelligence Ware, Inc.). In our own research we tried to use a knowledge acquisition program and found it unsatisfactory.[7] Instead, we have found far greater success using the face-to-face techniques for initial discovery of knowledge and knowledge structure that have been developed out of years of empirical research and theorizing in the social sciences. Many of these techniques derive from methods developed by anthropologists and linguists to learn the language and knowledge of their informants, often of a single "key" informant. These methods are objective and most often are verbal; they may or may not involve active participation of the investigator.

Since experts seldom even realize how much they know, much less how they structure that knowledge cognitively, direct inquiry is difficult. They frequently believe that they make their judgments on the basis of few rules, when, in fact, expert systems are likely to require hundreds to model rather minor domains of behavior.

Why might this be? And how can the developer efficiently obtain the needed information? In this section, we discuss these issues and present a set of methods for acquisition of knowledge, adapted from those anthropologists use in cross-cultural studies to access information.

Deep knowledge is probably never remembered accurately in the kinds of complete multilevel trees that frequently are used to represent relations among concepts. More likely, people probably create such trees (or parts of them) in the process of thinking about problems and their solution. Thus, the same expert may produce trees (or other "knowledge structures") that differ from time to time when attending to different distinguishing features. For example, in a study of the cognition of illness among Tojolabal Mayan Indians, Furbee and Benfer (1983) found that the importance that one couple assigned to certain aspects of their knowledge structures of illness varied, depending on whether their baby was ill.

In expert system development, trees of relations are created in the interaction between developer and expert. In a sense they are a joint product in that, to be successful in communicating ideas, the expert must cast them in a framework that both can be understood by the developer and can be translated by the developer into the expert system proper. The developer and the expert create a personal metalanguage through which they can discuss the evolving product representing the expert's knowledge structures.

The procedures in this section permit the developer to control the exteriorizing of the expert's deep, often out-of-awareness knowledge — the making explicit of some or all aspects of that knowledge to oneself and to another. When interacting, both participants in the process may conclude the exchange with a better comprehension of the way that knowledge is organized than either did initially. Both parties mutually negotiate the exteriorized forms that the expert creates. As this exteriorizing takes place, the expert will also learn about the methods and procedures that the developer uses, something that is necessary for that expert to participate fully as a partner. The developer must create a context that permits the expert to learn about the development activity itself; in so doing, not only will the expert be more helpful in the creation process, but he or she is also likely to be more adroit later at updating and revising.

Everyone has at least two kinds of knowledge about the world, including the social world of relationships, institutions, and interactions: (1) Knowledge that we know we know and (2) knowledge that is out-of-awareness. About the former, each of us holds a theory of the domains of knowledge and the way we structure that knowledge. We "know" English grammar. In fact, what we know explicitly about English grammar relates more to language usage and prestige styles of speaking and writing than it does to what we know that lets us speak and understand English. The last was mostly learned before we learned to read and write and certainly before we took up the *Chicago Manual of Style*. What we know we know about English grammar (or the political process, or engine repair, or medical diagnosis) is a metatheory of our explicit personal knowledge in that domain. Our highly personal metatheories about our knowledge at best explain our cognitions only partially, because although we often regard our in-awareness knowledge (and our metatheory of it) as everything we know, in fact, such knowledge is only a small fraction of total knowledge. Further, our explicit knowledge is largely trivial and public and reflects strongly the information we have learned in a formal, often classroom setting.

Our informal knowledge, on the other hand, is most often acquired by apprenticeship. It might be thought typical only of homely knowledge acquired at mother's or father's knee — how to ride a bicycle or how to hunt squirrels, for example — but in fact, it is exactly the way experts have learned the kind of knowledge that sets them apart. That knowledge is not what is taught in classes; it is what experience, from interactions with knowledgeable people in information-rich settings, has taught the expert. Since that knowledge is largely out-of-awareness, the experts either have no metatheory of it, or have a very limited and possibly highly individual one, and so tend to underestimate both how much they may know and how long and complicated will be the task of exteriorizing that knowledge.

The methods of **ethnoscience** offer an approach to the discovery of domains of knowledge from experts; they are based on structured interviewing and integration of tasks that tend to exteriorize knowledge. These methods depend very little on investigator and subject sharing assumptions. This chapter presents a set of these techniques adapted for use in accessing the knowledge of experts for expert systems development.

The Ethnoscience Approach

Early AI researchers hoped to develop a computer program able to emulate — possibly surpass — the human ability to solve problems, but investigation quickly dashed those hopes. Even a very simple "world," one comprised of geometrical shapes, proved impossible to manipulate without extensive knowledge of that world. One strand of AI followed that trail and used many ideas derived from linguistics; by limiting study to very narrow domains, it proved possible to specify enough facts and relations to solve limited but interesting problems. Expert systems today are the result. Like the field of artificial intelligence, anthropology was also influenced strongly by linguistics. In the 1960s anthropologists began to visualize understanding culture as like a language. Preliminary success at writing grammar-like rules for narrow domains, such as kinship, led investigators to enlarge the goal to include all of culture, to attempt to write a "culture grammar" (Colby, 1975), but this goal too proved intractible. Instead, very narrow subset "grammars" and "vocabularies" of domains were studies fruitfully. The anthropologist's methods developed for learning enough of the rules of a different people, often with an unfamiliar language, focused more on learning the key terms. In a sense, by concentrating on domains, rather than on an entirety, anthropology and artificial intelligence have developed mutually beneficial approaches. Ethnoscience offers expert systems development methods for knowledge acquisition; expert systems provides anthropology (and other social sciences) a creative way to link rules to behavioral outcomes.

The relatively assumption-free approach of ethnoscience is grounded in a distinction borrowed from linguistics, that between **emic** vs. **etic** analyses.[8] When an investigation seeks to model knowledge and behavior in terms of categories and structures that are congruent with the point of view of the group or individual being investigated, then that study is **emic**. For example, the folk expert system, FAI-SOILS, models the way farmers in the Colca Valley of Peru classify soils. As it turned out, those farmers use a classification system that relies on the friability (i.e., ability to be easily crumbled) and water-holding properties of a soil as primary distinctions. They combine their knowledge of soils types from the classification with knowledge of influences from microclimates (e.g., terraces, low flat fields, availability of irrigation water, frost risk, and so on) to arrive at cropping and management decisions that maximize the productivity of their holdings. Their knowledge of crop management was modeled in a second folk expert system, FAI-CROPS. Both were used to understand the indigenous knowledge of this group of Andean farmers, who are engaged in successful terrace agriculture, toward the goal of disseminating that knowledge to other Andean agriculturalists in similar environments who are less successful. In addition, by coming to learn the Andeans' point of view, it was hoped that we would provide a way to relate their system of knowledge to that of the Extension Service and other developmental personnel, whose ideas might be said to be Western or "modern." Interestingly, once it had been described emically in the Andean farmers' terms through FAI-SOILS, it became evident that the Andeans' soils classification system resembled closely one of the Western classification systems, that based on the texture of the soil.

On the other hand, had we attempted to describe the soils and actions of Andeans in terms of the Western classification of soils only, we would have been engaging in an **etic** study, one that is externally grounded. Etic studies ask questions of data that may be of little or no relevance to the persons from whom the data are drawn. For example, census questionnaires are often etic; the persons being interviewed have not been involved in the design of the questionnaire or the study, nor are they usually concerned directly with the report from it. Many clinical studies in medicine are also etic, since they are informed by a theory of disease causation that is seldom understood in its specifics by the subjects under investigation, and since the goals of such studies are usually not those of the patients. Recently, we have seen a conflict between these conflicting goals of investigators and subjects in the design of clinical trials of drugs to combat AIDS.

The key to modeling the deep knowledge that our experts hold will be to identify terms, concepts, and features of organization through interviewing and through various sorting tasks — to grasp even a small piece of a larger, more complex issue. Then having exteriorized part or all of one important piece of the expert's knowledge, the matter can be investigated further, using these methods, teasing out successively greater amounts of knowledge about the idea from the expert always in relation to what one learned at first and always with revisions of that first understanding in mind.

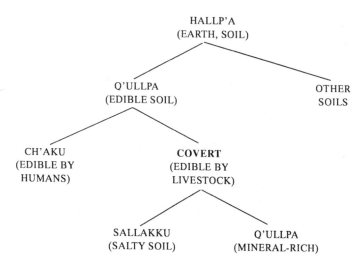

Figure 3.1. Taxonomy Showing Absence of Named Category for Mineral Soil that is Edible by Livestock, an Important Covert Category in the Cognition of an Andean Agriculturalist

As mentioned previously, some concepts are known by name (are overt), and some are not—they are covert. An example of part of a taxonomic tree showing a covert category (mineral-rich soils that are fed to livestock) is shown in Figure 3.1.

This tree derives from interviewing conducted with an Andean farmer as part of the construction of the expert system (FAI-SOILS) that models the classification of soils by terrace agriculturalists in highland Peru. As is frequently the case, the covert category only became evident to the developer and indeed to the expert as well, through examination of relations among named concepts, when the expert realized that there is a gap in the structured relationships among members of a set of terms. One of the best ways of discovering such covert categories is through the method of **general sorts** (also called "pile sorts"), and that was the method used to derive the taxonomic tree shown in Figure 3.1. General sortings are unconstrained divisions of sets into subgroups, followed by further division of those subgroups until no more groupings can be made by the expert. The developer keeps records of the membership of groups at each level and, after the expert has completed the task, asks about the reasons for creating the groups. In this way features of similarity among groups can be identified; indeed, the expert may be made aware of such features for the first time. The method of general sorting helps the expert exteriorize out-of-awareness knowledge and place it in the realm of knowledge of which he is aware, facilitating discussion of it. (General sorts is described more fully later in this chapter.)

There are some external criteria that can help a developer know when something is missing, even a covert category. One of these, **neutralization**, derives from the **theory of markedness**, a theory which predicts that with pairs of elements in opposition to one another, one member of the opposition — the **unmarked** member — will be more widely distributed or important, and often more in awareness. For example, in Figure 3.1 above, the feature of **human** predominates over that of **livestock**, and in fact can be expected to be unmarked universally. The same can be said for certain other categories; for example, the grammatical category of **singular** number is more common — is unmarked with respect to **plural** number. What is notable about these is that the unmarked member of such oppositions will in some instances stand for both categories: For example, a singular can represent a plurality, as in "The committee is in agreement." That is to say, the contrast in the opposition (singular/plural) is **neutralized** in the direction of the unmarked.

Knowing that such contrasts may be neutralized is a valuable aid to the developer in teasing out covert categories. Another useful technique is that of **scenarios** (discussed fully farther on in this chapter). In this technique, the developer presents the expert with a scene — a context — for use of an idea or term, and the expert may then correct or amplify the scenario. Equally useful is a request for scenarios (perhaps examples of use of a concept) from the expert, which the developer can then alter little-by-little to probe the limits of applicability of an idea or practice.

The fact that all social knowledge changes constantly in ways that are not obvious presents a profound problem for the development of social science expert systems. We cannot freeze social behavior or the knowledge that underlies it; rather, we must factor in some dimension of time. We must also recognize that even within a fairly homogeneous community, there will be variation in viewpoints. Chapter 5 addresses directly some ways of incorporating multiple viewpoints in an expert system. Finally, we must constantly keep in mind the effect of attitudes, beliefs, and values on the opinions of persons within social settings. These factors may change from situation to situation. Suppose we have a rule like the following:

Rule A.
If nutritional state is deficient,
and patient is frail and has difficulty swallowing,
Then employ iv feeding. **CF** = 90

The expert may regard a particular treatment such as the one in Rule A as correct and proper for a frail patient in a hospital or nursing-home setting and may do so with a confidence factor (CF) of, say, 90. The very same expert, however, may judge that action as hopelessly complex and unwieldy in the home setting. The context will dictate the expert's evaluation of the necessity of employing the treatment. In effect, the setting will alter the value of the expert's confidence factor for the applicability of a particular rule, creating a **metarule** that will govern the application (or firing) of Rule A and perhaps other rules pertaining to similar treatments.

Metarule A
If Rule A . . . Rule n is/are applicable,
and setting is home,
Then change value of CF for employ iv feeding to 20.

Thus we see that the rules of the expert system can themselves be governed and constrained by metarules. Those metarules may affect applicability, as does the one in our hypothetical example, or they may alter the form of a rule.

Knowledge Acquisition Methods

Ethnoscience techniques involve eliciting, in the native language (or the expert's argot), the names of items or categories (**terms**) in a **semantic domain**; examples of such domains include illness, material goods, soil types, folk veterinary practices, types of health practitioners, kinds of health care, colors, anatomy, and crop management practices. Also elicited are appropriate questions (**frames**) about the terms with which to learn culturally relevant information about the terms. Terms are collected by asking a question such as "What kinds of soils (or crops, or colors, or illnesses, or trade routes, and so forth) are there?" until no more terms are forthcoming. Alternatively or additionally, elicited terms may be compared by the native consultant using sortings and other kinds of manipulative tasks. Such tasks create comparative similarities among the terms that reveal the structure of the domain. They also yield named and unnamed attributes that can become the basis of questions and provide a scaffold on which the investigator can organize deeper inquiry into the cognitive arrangement of the knowledge. In this way, the investigator proceeds from a minimum of external assumptions, and the expert determines relevant materials and comparisons for study. There are available some computer packages that guide acquisition knowledge automatically, for example, ETHNO, but none covers all of these methods. Further, although they are useful, they ought not to be substituted for the interaction of developer and expert since it is in that context that a common metalanguage and mutual understanding are achieved. Some of these techniques are also described and illustrated in Spradley (1979) and Weller and Romney (1988).

Recalling that the **emic/etic** distinction can be simplified to mean "insider's" (**emic**) point of view vs. "outsider's" (**etic**) point of view for use in knowledge science, it is clear that developers of expert systems are engaged in **emic** investigations in that they are trying to capture "insider" knowledge from the "insider's" point of view. Implementation may or may not be **etic**, depending on whether there is an attempt to structure the expert system from the expert's perspective. It is easier to maintain a system that is intuitively "correct" to the expert — one that is **emic** — than one that is not. In addition, experts will feel that less violence has been done to their knowledge, that the expert system represents that knowledge, and they will be more positive about the enterprise and more cooperative.

To illustrate this approach to knowledge acquisition, we draw on our own work for examples. To lay out the whole package we start with the development of MUckraker, an expert system to model the process of expert investigative reporting for reporters and editors (see Table 1.1 for a small fragment of MUckraker). We wanted to know how an expert investigative reporter researches documents, and how that person obtains and handles interviews with persons who serve as sources for a story. We wondered whether different kinds of stories required different investigative activities. Furthermore, we were concerned with how expert reporters integrate and relate information from the document search and the interviews. Our first task was to learn the vocabulary of investigative reporting. To do that, and to learn the organization of that knowledge, we relied upon **elicitation, sortings, survey-type interview, ranking, props,** and **scenarios.** A selection of these tasks was first conducted with two expert investigative reporters who had somewhat different areas of expertise and experience.

Elicitation of categories and concepts. Most **categories** have names in a language, although rarely categories may lack a name, in which case, as we discussed above, they are called "covert." **Concepts,** on the other hand, often lack a conventional label, and the developer and expert must create a convenient vocabulary with which to refer to them. Since concepts are closely tied to actions, the task is essential. Beginning with elicitation of the more accessible vocabulary of categories, and using the result as a probe to tease out a vocabulary of concepts, the MUckraker project involved creating an expert system that involved both a set of categories (e.g., types of stories, issues, and activities) and a set of concepts (rules for obtaining, relating, and using information). We began with the simpler task, the one involving categories.

Names of types of stories were elicited from an expert investigative reporter by asking questions such as "What kinds (types) of stories (documents, issues, activities) are there?", "What are the names of the kinds of (documents, issues, activities) in preparing a particular kind of story?" More than 60 terms were collected in this way. These were cross-checked and verified with other experts and with the same expert on different occasions. In that way, we eliminated several terms, usually because they were synonyms or descriptive elaborations ("rapport" = "frequency of contact with source," "fairness" = "ethics"). We retained some descriptions because they seemed to be labels, often for higher nodes in a taxonomic tree. The total group was reduced by choosing what appeared to be the most widely known name from a group of synonymous terms. In this manner, the number of terms was reduced to 57, on which there appeared to be agreement, for use in the general sorting task. When it came time to elicit concepts, procedures were less straightforward. We will have more to say about that process below, but the use of **question frames** permitted us the first look at the structure of concepts about categories.

When the investigator is certain that a question, such as an elicitation question, is meaningful, it can be used over and over with slight modification to probe the domain of knowledge further — it can be regarded as a question frame. For example, from

"What kinds of sources are there?", there might develop eventually, question frames such as "What kinds of good sources are there?", "Is ____ (e.g., city clerk, former spouse) a good source?", "Is ____ always a good source?", "Can ____ be made into a good source by trading a favor?", "Is ____ a good source only when he/she is not personally involved?", and so on. Modifications must be checked, of course. One needs to know that the distinction being questioned is a valid one — say, for example, that between "good sources" and "bad sources," or between "kinds of information that are exceptions to rules" and "honest mistakes" — so the idea of a question about that distinction is appropriate and the investigator is asking about something meaningful to the consultant. That distinction may not appear relevant to the investigator as an outsider. Little by little, new question frames are teased out through the interview process. They expand knowledge of both the inventory and the structure of conceptual knowledge, and they are themselves used to extend the investigation to other parts of the domain of knowledge. In this way, we can examine all aspects of the chosen domain of knowledge and can elicit other important information that can be cast in additional question frames. When the productivity of interviewing with question frames begins to wane, it indicates that one has bumped up against the limits of a domain, or at least against the limits of an individual's knowledge of that domain, and it is time to try another means of eliciting knowledge.

General sortings. A general sorting task, also called a "pile sort" (Weller and Romney, 1988), is one way to learn how the vocabulary (categories) of a domain is organized. It also lets the developer identify covert categories and provides an excellent prop to use in discussing the organization of knowledge with the expert. In the MUckraker case, we put the 57 terms on slips of paper and drew them from a hat to approximate a random order. That gave a number for each term by which it could be quickly recorded. The terms (with code numbers) were then written on index cards, one per card. We gave the stack, in its "random" order, to an expert and asked him to arrange the cards in as many piles as he wished, according to any principle he wished, and told him not to concern himself with explaining to us what he was doing as he went along. He was asked to discard cards with names of stories, issues, or activities with which he was unfamiliar. Remaining inappropriate terms will be turned up at this time and can be clarified or eliminated. Sometimes additional categories are revealed at this stage also.

As soon as the expert reporter had divided up the 57 cards into groups, we recorded the members of each subgroup by number and asked him to divide any or all of the groups further, if he wished. In instances where he did make second-level subgroups, we recorded those by number and asked him to subdivide the second-level groups into third-level ones and so on until he said they could no longer be divided. We then went back through the tree implied from the sortings and, starting at the top, asked at each "node" on what basis he had decided to group things together or to separate them. Part of a sample tree developed from one such sorting, with labeled nodes, is given in Figure 3.2. The answers to these inquiries yielded a set of features or attributes that

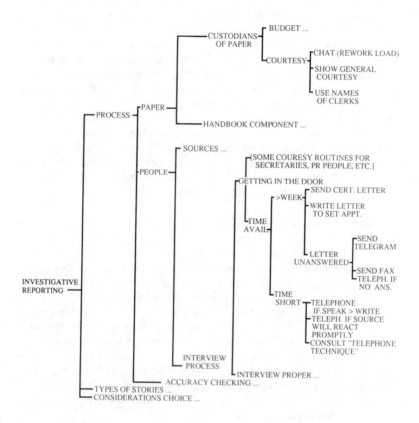

Figure 3.2. Partial Taxonomic Tree Derived from General Sorting of 57 Names of Kinds of Stories, Documents, Issues, and Activities Involved in Investigative Reporting by One Expert Investigative Reporter

characterized the various stories and reporting activities; these were convertible to a feature matrix of terms classified. The features, and discussions with the consultants about their decisions for each node, provided a list of properties of the terms and beliefs about them from which the questions could later be constructed for a survey interview.

Later when we have a complete prototype of the MUckraker expert system, we will ask the experts to perform a general sorting again but in this case with the print out of the screens of advice from the program. This late stage sorting will tell us the way the expert thought about the advice in the expert system and allow us to more closely mirror the expert's knowledge structure in the final program.

Rankings. Each reporter was also asked to rank his major groups, usually according to the sequence of events in order to determine the salience, or importance, of each item. For example, under the major heading of "getting in the door," choice of method of contact depended first on the amount of time available ("week or more" or "time short"); beyond that, initial contact methods were sequenced. For example, "send a certified letter" and "write a letter to set the appointment" were followed by things to do if the letter went unanswered ("send a telegram," "send a Fax"), and finally various telephone approaches. Rankings on the basis of some important feature (e.g., "reliability of information derived") can often help in working out confidence factors also.

Survey interviews. To extend the sample of information and to test how generally ideas were held by the community of experts at large, we have used survey interviews from the results of elicitations, sortings, rankings, and discussions of these with the experts. For example, for later development of MUckraker, an interview will be conducted with a wide sample of reporters based on the information derived from expert investigative reporters. For FAI-SOILS, the expert system for how Andean farmers classify their soils, we used an interview of 22 questions about 17 soil names. Most questions derived from the characteristics developed in discussions of the groupings resulting from general sortings of the 55 soil names in the study. From those 55, 17 soils names were selected to represent the range of major groupings (the taxonomic trees had an average of about eight major groupings) and to sample multiply within important groupings.

A survey interview takes considerable time to prepare, and it is tedious to complete, but it is very helpful when working in a situation which you understand poorly. Before modeling the understanding of an expert, who may or may not hold knowledge that is widely shared, the developer must check on how widespread a way of thinking is among members of the community of experts. The survey interview is also a check on how well the developer is coming to understand the problem; to make that check, the developer simply gives the survey interview to the expert or experts on whose knowledge it was constructed. The survey method, of course, may not be appropriate for problems where there are only a few experts or even a single expert.

Triadic sortings. Another way to check on the sharing of knowledge in the community of experts and on how well the developer is coming along in his understanding of that knowledge is to create a triadic sort. A selection of categories can be made that samples from important parts of the cognitive structure as the developer comes to comprehend it. Because this task involves creating all possible combinations of three among the items, and the numbers go up geometrically, no more than 12 or 13 terms should be used, unless one follows a balanced incomplete block design.[9]

The formula for determining the number is

$$\binom{n}{3} = \frac{n!}{3!\,(n-3)!} \qquad \text{where } n = \text{number if items}$$

For both MUckraker and the soils study, we used 12 terms. For example, for FAI-SOILS, we selected 11 soils from the 17 included in the survey interview to represent the range included in that interview and one additional one. All possible combinations of three among the 12 came to a total of 220 triads. The sequence of presentation within each triad was pseudo-randomized, and then the 220 triads themselves were pseudo-randomized for presentation in a triadic sorting task. The instructions for the task were to choose the two of the three soils in each triad that most resembled each other.

The results of this task give a matrix that is a measure of similarities among the categories, a matrix that can be converted to clusters or a tree structure. It can also be input to a variety of multivariate statistical procedures.[10] What one looks for in such results is replication of emerging cognitive structures and groupings according to the same attributes that experts used in making their general sortings. These are discussed in Chapter 5. In general, triadic sortings are especially useful as intermediate validation procedures. They help developers know that they are on the right track, and if not, where they have a problem.

Props. Having something concrete in hand helps elicit abstract ideas. A creative use of props also bridges the gulf from the easy elicitation of categories to the difficult elicitation of concepts or actions. In the Andean project, we had prepared two kinds of expert systems: One classified soils — an easy category project. The other modeled crop rotation and associated field management actions — a more difficult conceptual problem. One of the ways we moved from soil names to management decisions was through the use of props. For example, we took 13 actual soil samples collected by the soils scientist associated with the project, and asked local people to identify them by class, and to tell us information about each sample — for example, how one cultivated the soil, what crops grew well on it, where it could be found in the community, what other uses it might have, how much manure or other fertilizer a typical field of it would need, whether there was a difference in its management if it were in a terraced field or a large flat field, and so on. These discussions were often held with groups of experts rather than individuals, so we were privy to different opinions and the local experts' resolutions of disagreement. The information obtained went into a file of "concepts," different beliefs and practices associated with different soil types, where they joined the many pieces of information we had on attributes of soils collected through the sortings. Identifications of each soil sample provided another check on how much agreement there was in the community on soil classification. Since a soil scientist had also identified the soils in Western scientific terms (Sandor, 1989), the identifications of the local experts helped ultimately to relate the local soils classification (the insider **emic** system) to Western scientific classifications (the outsider **etic** system).

In another such task, we asked one of our local experts to draw a map of the lands controlled by the community and label different kinds of soils in them. This too provided a way for us to relate the local emic knowledge to outsider etic classification, since the soils scientist also prepared a soils map of the community lands (Furbee and Sandor, 1990).

For MUckraker, we used the taxonomic trees (e.g., Figure 3.2) from the sortings by experts as props for discussion by a "focus" group of interested parties — editors, reporters, and journalism professors. We found, for example, that there was disagreement among experts on how to seek an interview. Many thought that there was never time to write a letter, which led us to realize that the kind of investigative reporting conducted by the expert who was the author of Figure 3.2 — who primarily wrote books — differed vastly in its time constraints from that conducted by most of our target audience, newspaper reporters working on short deadlines.

Second level elicitation. As suggested earlier, eliciting concepts frequently involves the creation of a concept vocabulary, something that must be negotiated between expert and developer so both have a convenient set of labels by which they can refer to the actions that an expert takes and the conditions the expert considers in making decisions. These concepts eventually become additional content of rules, but the structure of those rules must be determined through joint discussion of relations, if it is to be faithful to the expert's out-of-awareness conception of the enterprise. Talking about **props** helps an expert verbalize how he or she uses knowledge, even if the props are no more than sketches of the emerging structures.

Scenarios. Once the developer has enough information to hazard guesses about the use of the knowledge, it is useful to create **scenarios** that involve situations in which the expert is asked to make one or more decisions. For example, in the MUckraker project we constructed situations in which the expert would have to move outside of his preferred mode of operation, and in so doing we learned some of the ways he broke (or bent) his own rules and which rules were more-or-less inviolate. That could inform our assignment of confidence factors for rules. In the Andean soil management study, we set up scenarios in which we asked our local experts what they would plant in a field given a certain set of conditions. A sample scenario might be the following:

If you were trying to feed a family of seven persons, what would you plant in a field that was, for example, a terrace, containing a certain kind of type soil with ample water, and located in a frost-free region; and if the family had six other fields, including some with very good, some with mediocre, and some with poor production possibilities? Then we would change some characteristic in the scenario, for example, the number of fields available to the family, or the number of family members, or the soil type. As we collected more and more answers to scenarios based on everyday field management situations, we began construction of the expert system modeling the crop rotation and field management. We were then able to use the evolving expert system to predict possibilities, that we could check with our local experts. The expert system itself became a prop for eliciting additional information, as well as an object to correct and enlarge.

Applications — Classification

Classification of soil is one important feature of the Andean farming system. Although a soils scientist was part of the team, we wanted to capture a system of classification which was **emic**, that is, meaningful to the farmers, independent of influences from Western soil science. This was necessary since the long term goal is to create an illustrated pamphlet version of the expert system to distribute to the many less successful Andean farmers, who are unlikely to accept totally foreign advice. Many international development projects have failed for this very reason.

In the Andean village, each farmer is an expert, farming land that has been in production continuously for as long as 1,000 years. Variation among experts is not usually error, in our view, but represents alternative strategies, or perhaps the range of variation that exists in the system. Multiple-redundant features might predict correct classification even where there are disagreements about some specific properties. There is a variety of methods for dealing with individual variation among experts, but we will focus on just two that we investigated for the Andean study.

Modal model. One previously mentioned method was to treat variation as error and select properties and soils for which there is good agreement for preparation of an expert system. According to this approach, a **modal** model (Table 2.3) was prepared by creating a spreadsheet where each entry represented the number of times each of four experts agreed with the characterization of a particular soil. The 1stCLASS shell was used to develop a quick representation. The limited inductive inference engine of 1stCLASS can be extended somewhat by creating products or sums of qualifiers with a spreadsheet program, but we used it directly in this case to see whether the properties we had elicited were sufficient to classify the soil types correctly. In order to have at least minimal validation in the field, the expert system developed from the first four informants was used to predict soil classes from the fifth: 14 out of 17 soils

TABLE 3.1 A Portion of a Multiple Pathways Model for Classifying Soils in Lari, Perú

Is the soil **soft?**
   yes: **white?**
      yes: **one of the best?**
         yes: **sandy?**
            yes: then the soil is **usp'a hallp'a** (2 consultants)
            no: then the soil is **usp'a hallp'a** (1 consultant)
                               or **qhilli** or **lamosa**
         no: **silty?**
           yes: **grows maize?**
              yes: then the soil is **qhilli**
              no: **sandy?**
                  yes: then the soil is **hallp'a**
                  no: then the soil is **kuntayu**
         no: **sandy?**
            yes: then the soil is **qhilli**
            no: **clayey?**
                  yes: then the soil is **yuraq hallp'a**
                  no: then the soil is **qhilli**
      no: **needs fertilizer?**
         yes: **sandy?**
            yes: **grows maize?**
              yes: **silty?**
                  yes: then the soil is **ñutu akku**
                  no: **stony?**
                      yes: then the soil is **ñut'u akku** or **akku**
           no: **stony?**
            yes: then the soil is **akku** (2 consultants)
           no: then the soil is **akku** (1 consultant) or
                           ñut'u akku
         no: **one of the best?**
           yes: then the soil is **hallp'a** (3 consultants)
           no: **silty?**
              yes: then the soil is **ñut'u akku**
              no: **grows maize?**
                  yes: then the soil is **usp'a hallp'a**
                  no: then the soil is **akku**

---

were correctly classified; the three errors were interpretable as owing to different experience of our experts with those soil types.

Multiple pathways model. We constructed a second model (Table 3.1), using the assumption that each expert probably had a difficult, possibly non-monotonic set of heuristics, which nonetheless could probably correctly classify soil. To give an example nearer to home, some Americans use the term "first cousin once removed" for the same relative that others would call a "second cousin." Careful study of these two systems reveals that use of the first term is motivated by generation, and of the second by laterality (Rose and Romney, 1979). The two systems produce similar maps of kinsmen, except for this one relative. Either is valid. Knowing that both exist would help a non-expert, i.e., a foreigner, understand how to classify kin in America. So, for the soil case, we created a matrix where each expert's responses to the frames for each soil were entered and weighted equally in what we call a Multiple Pathways Model. Again, as a rough and ready test of validity, we used the first four local experts to construct the model and entered the responses of a fifth as a test vector in 1stCLASS. Rather to our surprise, there were no errors in the sense that none of the 17 soil types was incorrectly classified, although many were classifiable only to a group of very similar soils. The last expert was not exactly like any one of the first four. But for each soil, his response was close enough to at least one of the previous four to result in a successful classification.

Applications — Taking Action

The Andean system of agriculture has depended upon a complicated system of crop rotation and fallow that has permitted soil to increase over the past 10 centuries. Soil classification is one part of Andean agricultural knowledge, an essential variable in cropping. Soil names may function as shorthand descriptions of features that separate agricultural soils from nonagricultural. For agricultural soils, soil names convey information about their possible use. Armed with the ability to classify soil correctly, we turned to learning how to manage crops.

Cropping decisions. Crop choice is a much more complex topic than soil classification. The major issues in crop choice revolve around the soil type, or types, in a particular field, and the previous crops planted there. The expert systems we constructed for each expert showed considerable individual variation in ideal cropping, even for a relatively small set of factors said to be important. Several strategies were involved in developing a combined set of rules. One was obvious: include rules that all, or nearly all, informants mentioned, and about which there was no disagreement. A trivial case would be rule number 12 of a 346-rule model:

If the soil type is *kuntayu* or *q'ullp'a*
Then don't plant anything.

These soil types are not really agriculturally productive and were included in the study to provide an "anchor" that might help integrate the other soils.

A more generally useful strategy was to use individual differences to provide estimates of "confidence factors," our confidence that where the If conditions were fulfilled, the Then would follow. For example, consider Rule 9:

If the soil is first class
    and the soil type is not *greda* or *kaskahal*
    and the field is a terrace
Then plant *maize* — confidence factor = 20/100

The 20/100 was obtained by finding the proportion of times the **If** conditions were followed by the *Then* in the rules elicited from the consultants. Its interpretation might be that 20% of the farmers of the village would make this choice 100% of the time. Or, any one of the farmers might choose this probability 20% of the time, depending on other circumstances.

The multiple pathways prototype worked fairly well. It is being perfected in a step-by-step design where different sets of farmers' recall data are used to test and improve on the weights originally developed from the interview data, bearing in mind that recall data are problematic (Bernard et al., 1984).

Other heuristics that will make the model more realistic include considerations of water availability, need and availability of fertilizer, and numbers of fields available to the family for cultivation. We will test the sensitivity of the model by simulations in which critical confidence factors are allowed to vary to see how much variation can be permitted before the crop choice is no longer specified correctly.[11]

For AI-FORENS, the set of expert systems to help forensic experts estimate sex and age at time of death from the hip bone (*os coxae,* or innominate bone), we also followed procedures similar to those we used in the Andes, even though we were dealing with fellow Americans, and even though one of us is somewhat of an expert in this area. We attempted to capture an **emic** representation of the bone for each expert. We elicited the named reference points on the bone that experts used in determining age and sex, and we had each expert sort these. We found it useful to ask the expert to "talk" his and her way through the identification of sample bones, and the use of different bones as props prompted the expert to think of additional instances or types of actions. We watched carefully how an expert handled a bone (we even videotaped the process), and in so doing, we turned up a couple of unnamed reference points (covert categories) on the bone. Preparing a prototype of a hundred rules took only a few days rather than a few months, as did the Andean expert system.

The goal for such studies is a model of knowledge acceptable to the experts, exactly the goal of the anthropologist who labors to understand "foreign" concepts in an unfamiliar "language." The techniques described here help expert and developer achieve a metalanguage that expedites the developer's modeling of the expert's knowledge in a congenial fashion. These methods should be particularly useful in developing a prototype, and since the prototype will be **emic**, it should be a good kernel for the development of a fully operational expert system. It may be, of course, that the knowledge engineer does not want to produce an **emic** system. As previously mentioned, one of the experts in the forensic study insisted that the way he solved forensic problems was that he considered all logical combinations of a series of qualifiers, a process that would have involved several thousand possibilities. We agreed with him that that was probably the way he understood the problem, but asked if we could instead develop a system of weighted indices based upon the features, solely from the perspective of keeping the expert system small. He agreed and took the trouble to learn the logic of the math variables so that he could see that the results would be close to his own. Thus, learning enough of the expert's vision of his or her knowledge, even if large parts are not to be embedded in the expert system, may help establish rapport with the expert and keep him or her interested in the project.

4. PRAGMATIC STRATEGIES

Many pragmatic decisions must be made in constructing expert systems. Here we discuss some of the most important ones and some of the strategies we have found useful in resolving these problems. The issues to be considered include:

1) Summarizing and editing the knowledge base
2) Reducing the complexity of the knowledge base
3) Selecting a method for handling uncertainty
4) Deciding whether to use an inductive or deductive approach
5) Choosing representation and inference strategies
6) The expert system development process

These issues apply to all expert systems. However, since most expert systems shells and most expert systems currently available are rule-based, in the interests of space, we focus most of our discussion on such rule-based systems.

Strategies for Summarizing and Editing the Knowledge Base

In rule-based expert systems, the structure of the knowledge is not fully represented by a simple listing of the rules. Backward-chaining is commonly used to select choices, in which instance the rules are not required to be in any particular order. Forward-chaining systems test rules in a set order and so will give some suggestion to the underlying structure of the logic of the system. Arranging the rules in order, perhaps in clusters or modules, helps one understand the system better and to facilitate debugging and maintenance. It is essential that rules be conceptually well organized.

Most expert system shells provide a way to organize and examine the impact of rules. These are often trace facilities that show which rules were used and the sequence of actions taken, along with facts that became known at each stage. Such facilities are sometimes inelegant, however; for example, in ESE, a mainframe expert system, the trace can be hundreds of lines long.

For organizing and editing rules, we recommend using decision trees, flow charts, decision tables, conditional decision tables, pattern representations, and rule tables.

Some of these methods are available in expert system shells. Others are not yet automated.

Decision trees. A decision tree is a representation in which the nodes mark alternative pathways, and the end-points, the final choices. This organization is an attractive one for any problem that can be phrased in a strict hierarchical form. Graph theory can be used as an underlying theoretical motivation. A desirable feature of decision trees is that their structure is simple and easily grasped visually. However, selecting such a method brings along several disadvantages, problems not always obvious to the neophyte knowledge engineer. In the first place, a decision tree is strictly hierarchical, whereas most problems are heterarchical, that is, there are multiple pathways from the top to the same node or final choices as in our Multiple Pathways Model (see Chapter 5). Second, decision trees do not ordinarily convey information as to how one might retreat up a now recognized false limb. Expert systems permit changing previous values in light of new information, a more realistic methodology. In any but the narrowest of domains, few instances of expertise come to mind that can be modeled completely by a simple decision tree. However, at a broader level, decision trees may be useful for mapping out the overall relations among sets of rules. They are also helpful in constructing parts of a knowledge base that can be represented in a tree-like structure. A well-known example of using a decision tree for selecting the correct statistical technique is provided in the booklet published by the Institute for Social Research (Andrews et al., 1981). Some expert system shells, such as VP-EXPERT or Nexpert, can display a decision tree that either reflects the entire problem or shows only the rules which actually fired in a recent run. Figure 4.1 shows a decision tree created by the VP-EXPERT program. The tree can be displayed in an overview form with just the graphic lines represented or in a close-up in which the actual variables are displayed. While this is a kind of decision tree, it should be remembered that expert systems, such as VP-EXPERT, permit *retracing a path* up the tree, when *two or more pathways* can lead to the same conclusion, and looping through the structure is possible. Thus, expert systems are a superset of the rules by which most decision trees are created and employed in making choices.

Flow charts. Flow charts have many of the advantages of decision trees, but more naturally permit recursion. The disadvantages are that most expert systems will be too complex to display in such a two-dimensional representation. However, a flow chart application with hypertext (described in Chapter 1) capability might be able to represent most expert systems efficiently. Flow charts are useful for visualizing relations among sets of rules. For example, there are 12 subunits of AI-CROPS (soil type, previous crop, type of field, and so forth), which we found useful to keep track of in a flow chart. Like decision trees, flow charts may be most useful when writ large in the management of individual units of expert systems.

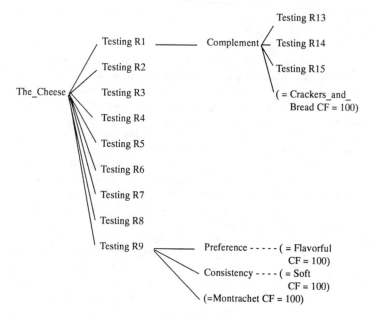

Figure 4.1. Graphics Tree Trace (after an example in VP-Expert)

Decision trees as decision tables. Decision trees can be rewritten as tables. Although they lose some of their graphic punch, they become more useful in developing expert systems. Creating a spreadsheet of examples for induction of rules for deduction is a good way to begin development of an expert system. This tabular format (see Table 4.1) has several useful characteristics. For one thing, it helps one to consider exhaustively the combinations of rules. For another, it reveals duplicate rules. Using the sorting power of a spreadsheet, one can view the rules organized by different antecedent sets, or by different sets of choices. However, a decision table presentation really permits one to deal effectively with only three, or at most four, combinations of antecedent conditions. This fact suggests that one should break the domain into subdomains during development, where each subset of rules can be developed and managed in a decision table format. The example in Table 4.1 above is a simplified example where the rows are rules (or examples) leading to a choice in the final column, and the columns represent just one of the antecedent conditions.

A more complex statement of a decision table is conditional decision tables. Table 4.2 shows a representation where the columns represent combinations of antecedent conditions. This method is a convenient one for keeping track of complex rules. Many shells provide the user with the facility to utilize decision tables; in fact, it is the primary mode of representing decisions for inductive expert systems.

TABLE 4.1 Speadsheet Arrangement of Fragment of Soils Classification Expert System

	Color: black	Color: dark	Color: white	Texture: thick/heavy	Texture: stony	SOIL TYPE
Rule 1	1	0	0	1	0	Hallp'a
Rule 2	0	1	0	1	1	Arsillia
Rule 3	0	1	1	0	1	Akku
Rule 4	0	0	1	0	1	Kuntayu

SOURCE: Adapted from Table 1, Furbee, 1989.

Pattern representations. An inference system may use both rules and pattern recognition to reason about a knowledge base. Frame-based systems often rely upon some form of pattern recognition to identify the appropriate frames for particular cases. Rule-based systems can also be used to implement a pattern recognition strategy. Pattern recognition may be essential when there are so many possible combinations of conditions that explicit rules to handle each would be too numerous. We have mentioned the ability of multidimensional scaling to find a structure and pattern in data obtained from multiple consultants. A spatial configuration can be obtained for a decision tree by multidimensional scaling (Tschudi, 1988); alternatively, it is possible to deduce a tree-like structure from a multivariate spatial representation (Furbee and Benfer, 1983). Multidimensional scaling (Kruskal and Wish, 1978) and cluster analysis (Aldenderfer and Blashfield, 1984) have been contrasted with multiple regression regression analysis (Lewis-Beck, 1980) in the development of expert systems (Brent et al., 1986; Tshudi, 1988). We will show in a later example that where there are multiple experts, regression weights from multiple regression analysis can be used to weight vectors discovered in multidimensional scaling. Such vectors can be recast as weighted variables in the expert system (see Chapter 5 for the AI-MOMS example that predicts when women will first present themselves for prenatal examination). In another study, AI-CROPS (crop management in the Andes), we have used individual differences multidimensional scaling (Arabie et al., 1987) of conditional decision tables (Table 4.2 presents a fragment of one conditional decision table) to find similar vectors and clusters of features to help us reduce the number of rules.

Another kind of pattern important in expert systems is the production of a profile, or pattern of antecedents associated with specific conclusions. STATISTICAL NAVIGATOR™ uses a pattern recognition strategy to select among statistical techniques, computing a summary score expressing the fit of each statistical procedure to a problem, then ordering procedures by their fit to identify the best procedures for a specific problem. A much simplified example of pattern representation is provided in Figure 4.2, in which the patterns of three different analysis techniques can be

TABLE 4.2 A Conditional Decision Table for Managing Subsets of Complex Rules

	IF first crop & terrace & soil is Uspa Hallp'a & farmer #III	IF first crop & pampa & soil is Uspa Hallp'a & farmer #III	IF first crop & terrace & soil is Akku & farmer #III	IF first crop & pampa & soil is Akku & farmer #III	IF first crop & terrace & soil is Llinke & farmer #III	IF first crop & pampa & soil is Llinke & farmer #III
THEN plant with confidence factor:						
CORN	60	0	0	0	0	0
POTATO	0	0	0	0	0	0
PAPAS LISAS	30	0	0	0	0	0
BROAD BEAN	0	100	70	70	100	100
MILLET	0	0	0	0	0	0
WHEAT	0	0	0	0	0	0
OCA	10	0	0	0	0	0
PEAS	0	0	30	30	0	0
ALFALFA	0	0	0	0	0	0
TARWE	0	0	0	0	0	0

contrasted to the pattern of objectives and assumptions of the user for a particular problem. Pattern recognition programs essentially examine these patterns to find the best solution to fit the problem.

Reducing the Complexity of the Knowledge Base

The developer may be overwhelmed by the number of combinations of antecedents experts claim to consider. Some experts discuss, for example, a classification system as if it were a paradigm — the cartesian product of all possible antecedent values (Degerman, 1972). In practice, many of the cells so defined are probably empty, and in any case, since their number grows geometrically with the number of conditions, it is not possible to elicit all the values from the expert. Even in a simple case, where every antecedent conditions has only two values, there are 2^n combinations of these for each choice. A number of different strategies are available to deal with this problem.

Intermediate values. It is usually possible to break the expert system into intermediate results that can be combined to produce the final choice. For example, as mentioned earlier, one expert in the AI-FORENS project maintained that he considered all combinations from a large number of factors. We persuaded him to accept instead a weighting scheme in which weights for each sub-set were awarded, and these intermediate values were combined in a formula acceptable to him.

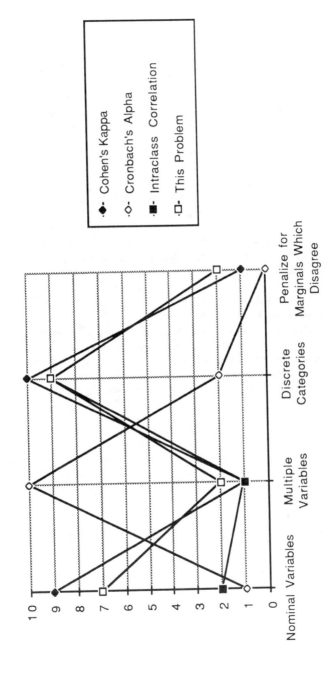

Figure 4.2. Pattern Recognition Example

Multivariate procedures. In most instances, the expert can agree that many potential combinations do not, in fact, occur and that they can be assigned a choice such as, "No advice for this combination." However, even with their elimination, the problem space may still remain very large. In this case, application of multivariable and multivariate statistical methods can reduce redundancy in an efficient manner. Two procedures, multiple regression and nonmetric multidimensional scaling have been discussed above. Other procedures, such as cluster analysis, could also be used in a preliminary attempt to reduce the number of logical combinations. These patterns are discovered by working with the expert. Even though the expert may not have these patterns in conscious awareness, such representation of the knowledge may not violate the expert's understanding of the domain if it is done properly. In fact, we find that experts are usually very interested in these representations and are quite able to discuss their possible significance for the task. The emic perspective of the expert often consists in large part of an episodic or routinized component, which is outside of awareness. However, the knowledge acquisition methods described in Chapter 3 help reveal this knowledge; multivariate analysis of those data may help reduce breadth to just the domain of interest.

An expert system should probably have several layers of partial redundancy built in to avoid error due to a single "mistake." The developer must strike a balance between too many logical combinations and a parsimonious representation that merely captures the flavor and feel of the task. Naturally, a parsimonious model that is validated to be very successful is highly desirable. The question is, what are the costs of errors? In medical diagnoses, the cost may be very high. But where the expert system is designed to capture only the most important elements, the heuristic value of a simpler system may be more important than improving prediction a final 10%.

Selecting a Method for Handling Uncertainty

Confidence factors present a problem unique to expert systems management because of their effect within a rule and across rules through the combination of rules that reach a common conclusion. An excellent and compact introduction to this topic is found in Ng and Abramson (1990). Several moderately priced shells provide a mix of methods. VP-EXPERT, for instance, uses fuzzy logic (Negoita, 1985) in OR statements and treats AND statements as independent probabilities. The Intelligent Developer treats the joining of two facts in the **If** part of the rule by OR (and XOR (exclusive or), +, and –) as dependent probabilities, but AND (and *, /, mod/ or ^) as fuzzy independent. While this is a reasonable approach, the developer needs to create a few simple examples and observe the behavior of the confidence factors to become familiar with these properties. EXSYS permits confidence factors to be treated as if they were what it labels independent, dependent, or average probabilities, although its usage for the former two is idiosyncratic. Careful thought should be given to which of these methods is adopted. For example, if the expert system is one in which a series of heuristics, each with a relatively low confidence, can together approach near certainty, the average method will produce a disappointingly low final value; whereas, a better method would cause each contributing fact to increase the confidence factor by its confidence factor multiplied by what remains between the present confidence factor and certainty. The fuzzy or minimum of the set of confidence factors may be more appropriate when the expert seeks to minimize a wrong choice, for example, in prescribing medicine. Moderately priced shells differ in the control they permit the user. If, instead of using the methods for manipulating confidence factors supplied with the shell, one wants to select other methods (perhaps differing in different parts of the expert system), it is generally possible to create mathematical variables to which are assigned some value, say between 0 and 100 (THEN Y = 50 rather than THEN Y, CF = 50, for example). These variables can be combined according to the formula furnished by the user in a special rule for that purpose (for example, **If Y < Z Then** conclusion). This method was illustrated in the MUckraker example in Chapter 1. For rapid prototyping, the default values furnished may be useable, but we prefer the control that variables give us over confidence factors.

Deciding to Use an Inductive or Deductive Approach

Inductive expert system shells attempt to create rules from examples. They are very useful where knowledge can be collected in a matrix form, often when the columns identify the conditions and the correct choice for each individual expert, whose data are organized by rows. Thus, the first column of an expert system to help one decide upon an appropriate expert system might be: "If more than $3,000 is available to purchase the system, and a complete development system is needed, then . . ." Each expert would fill in the cell, with, for instance, Nexpert. If the samples are well chosen, a simple algorithm (ID3), implemented in several expert system shells, will select an order and a minimum number of cells for which information may be needed.

Inductive approaches are typically only useful in expert systems for beginning stages. Inductive programs still do not approach the ability that human participant/observers have to deduce underlying rules. Tree structures are only useful at the broadest level, to organize constituent parts of an expert system, or at the very end of development for making fine distinctions. Productions rules, a deductive representation of knowledge, may begin with induction or contain subsets created by induction. If the problem is simple enough to be efficiently solved by inducing rules from well-selected examples, one probably does not need an expert system to find a solution. An inductive approach may be preferable when the experts tend to think about and talk about their work in terms of cases rather than abstract principles. For example, an inductive approach might be helpful when working with physicians or social workers, who may find it easier to talk about specific cases or patients than to talk about abstract rules. In such circumstances an inductive expert system shell that can work with cases to induce potential rules may provide a jump-start in developing the knowledge base.

Deductive models are the more flexible choice. They permit intermediate values and common-sense reasoning; they also permit one to change previously reached conclusions on the basis of new evidence. They allow confidence factors in antecedent conditions, in conclusions, and in the over-all strength of the rule. Any real problem is almost always best approached through deductive models.

Choosing Representation and Inference Strategies

Selecting an appropriate representation strategy for a problem is a crucial decision which greatly influences the difficulty of performing various kinds of reasoning about the problem. As a result, some representation schemes appear "natural" and easily applicable to a problem, while others make it difficult to express important concepts or perform common forms of reasoning used in the problem area.

By way of illustration, let us consider the two major methods of representation: rules and frames. Most of the programs discussed in this book, and most of those currently available, employ rules. We found rules to be a very natural representation for a wide range of phenomena, from selecting the appropriate procedures for designing research to classifying soils in Peru. However, when trying to represent the relatively sophisticated and complex qualitative theory of Erving Goffman, we found rules inadequate for the task. Much of Goffman's theory (and indeed, we suspect important aspects of many social science theories) involves hierarchical concepts. Trying to represent such hierarchical relationships as rules would have required us to create explicit rules relating each class of concepts. Although this operation is possible, it would be inelegant. In contrast, when we implemented this theory using a frame representation, the inheritance of properties from more abstract concepts could be efficiently implemented with only a few rules applying to all hierarchically related concepts. In short, we found frames to be far more efficient for representing varying levels of abstraction than rules.

Another class of problems for which frames appear superior to rules is that involving several different cases or units considered simultaneously. Rule-based systems generally favor consideration of a single event or case at a time and have difficulty comparing two or more cases simultaneously. Frames, on the other hand, explicitly recognize the possibility of multiple occurrences of particular combinations of features as separate "instantiations" of abstract conditions. Considering multiple cases or instantiations with rules has been a problem in several projects we have considered. In one project, where we attempted to use an expert system to schedule different physicians to cover several affiliated family practice clinics, the rule-based approach became extremely complex, at least in part due to the need to consider multiple actors and settings simultaneously. As with the Erving program, frames let us represent multiple actors or multiple settings with little trouble. MUckraker, begun with the simpler rule approach, will probably be implemented in a more frame-oriented representation.

The Expert System Development Process

Intelligent expert systems are not created overnight, rather they typically require a lengthy development process, during which an initial raw prototype is successively refined until it reaches an acceptable level of performance. There are a number of important strategies that can make this development process more fruitful. First, there is wide agreement in the literature that *prototyping is far superior to the traditional life-cycle development* for developing expert systems. An iterative approach minimizes "goal-slippages," the moving target sometimes presented by the user's changing needs.

The *prototyping strategy* (Waterman, 1986) begins with the programmer (in this case, the knowledge engineer) developing a crude prototype program that gives the user a view of how the program might look. Users then examine the prototype and suggest ways to improve its performance and correct its mistakes. The knowledge engineer then spends a few days or weeks making those incremental changes. This cycle is repeated until, eventually, there are few or no changes remaining to be made and the user accepts the program. The prototyping strategy may be particularly useful for expert systems when the users are unfamiliar with what programs can do for them and need a better understanding of how such a program might operate. Another important reason for using the prototyping approach is that substantive experts are typically unable to specify accurately how they actually perform their tasks, so the initial programs frequently perform poorly. Together, these factors make it important to develop expert systems using the prototypes and successive refinement cycles. Early in this process the program can be validated informally using hypothetical cases. As the program develops, validation of its performance becomes increasingly demanding, moving from hypothetical cases to a convenience sample of real cases, and finally to examining a representative sampling of cases.

5. MULTIPLE EXPERTS AND TESTING THE MODELS

Study of the organization of knowledge systems does not of itself necessarily lead to a model that predicts behavior. Statistical models, when used in concert with more structural multivariate models, can enhance design of a successful expert system. Such systems in which weights for the confidence factors are developed from statistical methods can both describe the organization of knowledge and predict behavior. Resulting expert systems can be superior to a simple predictive model by benefitting from knowing the underlying logical structure of a domain. Where prediction is as successful as that of an expert, *individual problem solving strategies* have been identified and operationalized. Validation is relatively straightforward in normative expert systems, such as HOME-SAFE-HOME. In the following discussion, we begin by listing some problems that inhere in assuming a single expert, or a single method

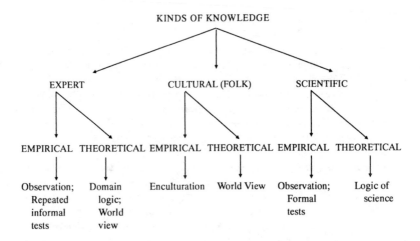

Figure 5.1. Kinds of Knowledge

of reasoning, and then discuss how more complex expert systems can be scientifically validated.

Knowledge that Adheres Among Multiple Experts

Figure 5.1 shows a knowledge tree that illustrates three ways in which knowledge may be understood. The first, the anthropological concept of cultural or "folk" knowledge, is that knowledge that is available to most members of an ethnic or social group. Folk knowledge has a "theoretical" component, which is the view of members of each society and their place in the universe, its world view (Kearney, 1984), and it depends partly on empirical observations, but the reasoning of folk knowledge may differ from that of logicians or members of other societies. Satisficing may be preferred to maximizing, for example. Even such a seemingly simple task as making inferences by class inclusion may be something that is not necessarily approached in a universal manner. Consider the answers to the following questions: 1. Is the nail a part of the finger? 2. Is the finger a part of the hand? 3. Is the hand a part of the arm?

If the reader's answer is yes to each, will you accept the conclusion that the nail is part of the arm? Most Americans will not. Indeed, there is evidence that there are limits to the depth of folk taxonomic trees for many classification systems in many societies (Randall, 1976). Or, to take another example, how many Americans will accept conclusions reached by *modus ponens*? Or the "no" returned to queries in

PROLOG when the answer appears indeterminate to most users? Analogous reasoning or metaphors (Lakoff, 1987) may be more important than principles of formal logic. Discovering the metaphors important to an expert may be a crucial if often neglected step in development.

"Expert knowledge," is generally the "folk knowledge" of an individual who has exceptional experience, probably with a feedback component permitting one to alter choices as new occasions are encountered. Thus, a knowledge of the underlying folk principles may be critical in understanding this knowledge and "improving" it towards greater predictive efficiency, if such is the goal. For example, since most people tend to overestimate the frequency of rare events, confidence factors may be overestimated for unusual occurrences. "Scientific knowledge" differs from "folk knowledge" and "expert knowledge" by the addition of "formal logic," or at least the logic in widespread use by scientists ("logic in use"), along with more stringent requirements for validation.

Nearly all previous studies in knowledge engineering have been developed with a single expert; standard texts make this assumption without even considering the case where the knowledge from a number of experts is to be modeled. In the special case where the knowledge really is largely held by a single individual, a specialist, existing expert system shells and standard procedures can be applied. But in general, we do not assume that much human knowledge is wholly held by a single person. The empirical question, in any case, is to what extent any domain of knowledge is shared.

Differences among experts may be modeled in a number of ways. One is to produce an individualized expert system for each, a strategy we have adopted for AI-FORENS. In that research, three experts were studied. Results will eventually be combined, and the combined system validated with a sample of known sex and age.

Individual differences have proved useful in measurement and structural studies. Multivariate procedures such as three-way scaling (Kruskal and Wish, 1978) and least squares fitting of one representation to another (Benfer and Furbee, 1989a) have used differences among individuals as a primary means to interpret the structures observed when individuals are pooled. Individual differences in organization of knowledge and in behavior related to a particular domain of knowledge may be viewed in one perspective as unexplained inter-observer error and handled by appropriately modified psychometric procedures (Cancian, 1963). Some of the procedures subsequently utilized (Romney et al., 1988) to solve some of these problems were originally developed as psychological tests, which are usually comprised of *novel* written questions concerning a variety of domains of knowledge; but these psychometric methods may be less appropriate for explaining differences in the knowledge of experts since the experts' knowledge concerns familiar topics. Selection of a proper sample of consultants is essential in any study of multiple experts, of course (Poggie, 1972). The domains studied in cognitively phrased ethnographic studies usually have been ones of exceptional interest to most consultants (Boster, 1986; Johnson, 1980), and one may anticipate differences in the character of the structure of knowledge held about domains depending on the degree to which they are of special interest to an individual or a society.

Basic groups (Rosch, 1978), the most essential categories, can be distinguished from less salient categories by the procedures outlined in Chapter 3. Occasionally, explainable differences may be related to perceptual limits in classification; for example, color blindness can affect a person's cognition of color. Other kinds of differences result because the consultant is describing fuzzy sets (Kempton, 1978; Boster, 1987), where degree of membership in a category is possible, even though the questions of the investigator and the responses of the consultants might suggest that set membership is absolute. Remaining individual differences might still be explainable by considering the differences as contributing to a possibly evolving pool of knowledge as perceived circumstances change. Or in a more social vein, rules of deference may determine the "correct" view in a particular group setting.

A possible direction for research would be to permit confidence factors to vary among informants in such a manner as to minimize the number of rules required. Where known examples exist, it might be possible to maximize successful prediction by iterative adjustment of these confidence factors weights. At present, more ad hoc methods may be employed.

Experts' expert systems. One straightforward approach is to model each expert separately. Performance testing then reveals which expert's knowledge is best for a given test data set. Such an approach might be considered when experts are few and isolated, so that little sharing is expected. Of course, comparisons of the underlying logic of each separate system might be revealing and suggest how the knowledge of different individuals might be combined.

Another method of combining this knowledge, practicable where a decision-table can be constructed which contains all possible combinations of rules, is to code each individual expert as one antecedent condition (see Table 4.2). For example,

Rule 1	Rule 2
If expert A	**If** expert B
and Condition 1	**and** Condition 1
Then chose XYZ, CF = 80	**Then** chose XYZ, CF = 35

A third method with which we have had some success is to enter the rules for each expert as independent rules in the same system.

Model I: Multiple Pathways. In this method, each rule in a person's model is considered as an acceptable pathway and weighted equally with all other consultants' possibly different rules. The motivation is that sometimes similar results can be obtained from somewhat dissimilar reckonings. Recall the example of different methods of reckoning kinship in the United States leading to nearly identical identification of relatives. The two methods proceed in slightly different order in the application of distinctive features (Rose and Romney, 1979). More redundancy might be expected in important domains (for example, cropping decisions), since imperfect learning or variable learning experiences might still produce good results. In this instance, the rules elicited from expert A and expert B above would be represented as:

Rule 1
If Condition 1
Then Choice X, CF = 85

Rule 2
If Condition 2
Then Choice X, CF = 80

While this approach might lead to contradiction, the particular trace through the backward-chaining system might lead to condition 1 from one consultant, but condition 2 from the other. A successful example (FAI-CROPS) of the method was presented in Chapter 3.

Model II: Modal Models. Another possibility we have discussed is to construct a model based on modal values that represents knowledge responses or observations (Young, 1981). Study of why a particular individual's outcome failed to be predicted may lead to improvements in the model. For example, if some grouping of consultants, say less experienced "experts," has more false predictions than most, perhaps the class "experience" should be entered as a variable in the system. Thus, multiple pathways can be discovered in the analysis of cases that do not fit a modal representation.

Model III: Statistical Determination of Weights for Heuristics. Another method we have used (also discussed in Chapter 3) is empirically to establish weights, or confidence factors, of the sort, **If X Then Y**, with a **confidence** of **80%**. One tabulates the number of times such a rule was mentioned by consultants to obtain the weight or confidence factor. In this procedure, deterministic rules are elicited from different consultants and subsequently weighted in the expert system by their frequency of occurrence.

Expert systems lend themselves naturally to studies where classification is at issue. Simple inductive trees can be developed with the expert, when time is precious, to provide preliminary models of the relationships among the categories. Moreover, entering different pathways as valid classifications permits examination of the character of individual differences in the field. The ability of these simple models to handle confidence factors also recommends them for studies concerned with possible differences among individuals.

Rule-based systems can contain facts (such as **X is a kind of Y**), and procedures, in the form of deterministic rules (**If X, Then Y**) or heuristics (**If X, Then Y** 80% of the time; or **If** X 70% of the time, **Then** Y 60% of the time). Moreover, intermediate results (**If X Then Y** 80% of the time; **If** Y > 75% of the time, **Then** Z) are necessary in any but the simplest systems. Decision trees are very useful structures (see Breiman et al., 1984), but knowledge usually depends on intermediate states of belief and conjectures as well as initial assumptions (Hart, 1986).

Specialists in expert systems tend to agree that the organization of knowledge is "the central determinant of effective use of knowledge" and that deep knowledge and problem-solving structures may require different knowledge-based expert systems to solve a particular problem (Chandrasekaran, 1988: 14). Thus, creation of a valid expert system for one domain may hold the basic dimensions of a model that would be useful in other domains. Individual differences highlight those assumptions that are shared and suggest different, possibly equally valid, structures which are related to important behaviors. Expert systems developed from responses elicited from different consultants are useful for at least the following reasons:

1) They may show the limits of elicited shared rules (e.g., a serious symptom to one expert might not loom as important to another).

2) They may point to alternative models that lead to dissimilar predictions (why does one farmer plant early, another late).

3) They may point to alternative models that lead to equivalent predictions (e.g., sail south to the African coast, then west to the Caribbean vs. sail south until the butter melts, then west).

4) They may show unexplained errors and misunderstanding between the developer and expert, but in study of domains highly salient to the consultant this explanation ought not be the first one considered.

5) They permit simultaneous analysis of the meaning and organization of a domain along with choices predictable from the model.

The knowledge of an individual expert has been the source of very specific applications in most existing expert systems; social scientists are more interested in using this knowledge in examining the context of a problem, as a means of guiding their research. Knowledge engineers have tended to exaggerate its importance, whereas most social scientists have tried to minimize individual human judgment when studying a phenomenon (Shangraw, 1987). We have found that consideration of the character of these differences holds one key to better understanding of the relation between heuristics supposedly useful in solving problems and the actual problem-solving strategies selected by an individual.

Testing the Model

Consistency and sensitivity. Consistency in an expert system is not a virtue if validity is diminished. Different components of a useful system may require different representations of knowledge. It may even be necessary to use different methods of combining the pieces of information, the facts. Some shells, such as KnowledgePro, offer built-in devices for relating differing representations, for example, frames as well as rules. Other shells such as Personal Consultant will permit representations using an AI language. Even less fully equipped rule-based shells can be adapted to allow smooth incorporation of varying representations within a single system. For example, by using different methods of combining confidence factors in different parts of the shell (see below), one can adopt the most favorable association (resolve a conflict set by selecting the rule with the maximum confidence factor) in one part of an expert system, while in another part of the same system allowing a different approach to obtain, such as permitting a series of facts, each to contribute to a final index score. In some sections of the knowledge base, it might be desirable to reconsider an earlier answer in light of a later conclusion (i.e., return to a node and begin again) or even change the earlier answer. An expert can jump to a premature conclusion, but based on the developing chain of evidence, he or she may come to "see" an earlier trait in a new light.

By sensitivity, we mean the likelihood that a conclusion will be altered by relatively slight changes in the confidence factors, or their mathematical equivalents. Thus, a robust expert system is one that will continue to give the same good results despite minor changes in the confidence factors. A very robust expert system will have heuristics that do not greatly depend on the system used to manipulate confidence factors. Simulation, where each confidence factor is varied and the performance of the system is evaluated, is a good method for finding "sensitive" branch points, where relatively slight changes in the confidence factors have major consequences in the performance of the system.

Building-in redundancy minimizes the sensitivity problem. Few experts in heuristic areas of expertise would permit their conclusions to depend on one fact or on one combination of facts. A better strategy would be to examine a variety of indicators so that one misplaced confidence factor will not degrade the system. Redundancy is an important issue, one that goes to the heart of how heuristic reasoning can lead to such a high level of performance. In general, one avoids an overly sensitive expert system, unless very high quality factual data are always available. Besides simulations, another approach for detecting weak links in the chain of reasoning is to interview multiple experts (Benfer, 1989). The range of confidence factors among a series of experts, however developed, may then help provide a minimum range of acceptable values, where the reasoning for each expert can be represented similarly. Sensitivity in confidence factors and their combination is one measure of the adequacy of the syntax of the model.

Testing of an expert system can be conveniently divided into two parts: testing the syntax of the code (the production rules) and testing the semantics, or adequacy of the representation of the knowledge of the domain. That is, one can look at an expert system as a higher level language whose code is the procedures (rules) and declarations (facts). The code is directed toward two ends: first, adequate prediction or choice or classification — the goals of the system, and second, representation of the knowledge adequate for communication with the expert and, one hopes, adequate also for the expert to participate in the development, maintenance, and evolution of the expert system. The code, or syntax, probably will not correspond precisely to the expert's understanding of the process, but the basic organization of the expert system should be recognizable by the expert as a transformation of his or her understanding of the domain. For example, a tree-like structure is represented by branching rules, or a recursive structure by nested rules.

Syntax has several meanings when applied to the code developed with the aid of an expert system shell. The meaning of *syntax* for a procedural language, such as BASIC, or PASCAL, is approximately homologous to its meaning for natural languages: Syntax is the permitted order of elements. While statements in a procedural language may appear to be in a linear order, as are words in a sentence, hierarchical and other organizations may be specified by them, and a syntactically incorrect expert system almost certainly will not produce useful results. However, even a syntactically correct expert system may still produce bad choices. An expert system that will produce valid conclusions might be said to be one in which the *semantics* are correct. By semantics we mean, for both natural languages and higher level computer programming languages such as expert systems, the combination of definitions of terms (as dictionary entries), according to rules (which may specify order, class inclusions, confidence factors, and other properties).

Validity is assessed by application of these rules to properly identified terms, the conclusions from which are judged correct or at least plausible by the expert. Alternatively, an expert system may be tested semantically with an adequate set of test cases, hypothetical, recalled past cases, or prospectively predicted instances.

The semantic, or meaning, component may hold the greatest potential power in representing useful knowledge, but it also presents a persistent problem in development. The problem is especially irksome to those with previous programming experience in algorithmic languages. The desire to maintain control may cause such a person extreme difficulty in taking advantage of the inference engine's ability to keep track of all possible interactions among rules. In a way, backward-chaining expert systems are rather like BASIC programs with very free use of GOTO statements; the intelligence in the system is that it keeps track of all GOTO statements and knows where to go next if the previous GOTO has led to a dead end.

Beginning expert system programmers with previous programming experience often try to fight the seeming loss of understanding of what the system will do by forcing an extreme hierarchical or tree-like structure on the knowledge-base. Forward chaining appeals to them since it appears to offer the programmer a way to keep track of the order in which every rule fires. Nonetheless, this task is not necessarily any simpler than keeping track of a backward-chaining system, where there are many rules and relatively few choices.

Looked at this way, to focus on the *syntax* of an expert system is to miss the chief virtue of expert systems, their *semantic* representation. For this reason we have argued throughout that an expert system, which is as faithful to the knowledge structure held by the expert(s) will be the simplest to develop and maintain in the long run. While a traditional programmer will attempt to translate the usually messy reasoning exhibited by the expert into spare, elegant code, experience shows that the translation is seldom successful, representing more of the programmer's knowledge, perhaps, than that of the expert.

Nevertheless, it is still essential to understand the syntax of each shell. Artificial intelligence languages such as PROLOG or LISP have a definite syntax. However, an expert system shell's ability to backward chain makes it difficult to detect some kinds of syntax errors, even though, as higher level languages, expert systems make it easier to maintain proper syntax due to the separation of the inference engine from the knowledge base. Tracing rule firings is necessary (see Chapter 4, Figure 4.1); however, it is also quite difficult to trace all the possible paths through a backward-chaining expert system. Commercially available shells vary in the help they provide. Debugging is best done with real examples, but hypothetical cases can also be useful where the set is designed to sample widely within the domain possibilities.

Keeping track of syntax presents different problems in the three major kinds of rule-based expert systems—forward-chaining shells, backward-chaining shells, and shells that permit both types of chaining by either separating rules into subsets or establishing a priority of which method is applied first. EXSYS, for example, permits true forward-chaining, which proceeds through the expert system rule-by-rule. It permits backward-chaining, where the first "choice" or consequent condition is examined first to see in which rule this choice is concluded, then tested to see whether the consequent conditions for this particular rule are true, possibly by examining other rules in which the consequent rules are concluded, and so forth. This linear approach is helpful in beginning to establish the skeleton of an expert system. Other shells, such as Intelligent Developer, permit either forward- or backward-chaining within subsets of rules, any set of which can be disabled. That most shells differ in the order of application of rules means that the developer has to study the manual carefully to see which syntax system she or he is employing.

Syntax errors may range from simple misspellings or inconsistencies in use of upper or lower case letters to loops or implied loops in the reasoning process. While any solvable problem can be represented by either a forward- or a backward-chaining system, as discussed in Chapter 1, forward, "exploring" systems may be more difficult to write code for, since all knowledge necessary for each rule must be present before that rule is interrogated. On the other hand, this necessity probably reduces the likelihood of bad syntax. In a backward-chaining approach is all too easy to overlook the implications of a rule, especially one added to an existing system. Expert systems shells are likely to evolve better syntax checking systems, such as the ability to detect loops and better representation of traces. Still, validation studies are the final arbiter of success in developing a syntactically and semantically useful expert system.

Validity

Some Examples of Methods Used in Validations. Validation is the most important aspect of the development of any useful expert system. Although most expert systems are developed in an ad hoc manner, following formal methods such as we have presented, one can achieve more theory-directed expert system development. In either instance, validation is critical as in all scientific models. Consistency is the critical issue at the stage of knowledge acquisition (Figure 5.2), and reliability (Figure 5.3)

ACQUISITION CYCLE

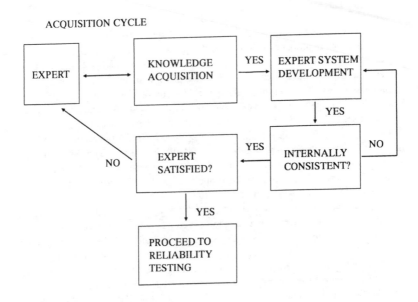

Figure 5.2. Establishing Consistency as Part of the Acquisition Cycle

can be assessed if multiple experts or multiple sessions with a single expert are available.

Once candidate models have been developed, whether they come from several experts or are versions of a single expert's model, one must give primary consideration to reliability (Figure 5.3).

Finally, at the point of testing the performance of the developed expert system, one must be involved with questions of true validation (Figure 5.4).

Simulation and Test Cases. Where test cases are available, the strongest test of validity is to select by probabilistic methods a subset of the available instances for testing and remove them from the development process. A special case is recall of previous choices. It is predictable that the farther back in time cases came to the expert, the more normative will be his or her recall of choice. This tendency can be used to advantage if the oldest cases are elicited first in order to create the first prototype. These older cases may be more meaningful to the expert in that they may represent more what we have called the semantic component than the episodic or routinized component of the expert's knowledge. For that reason, their explanation may be brought to conscious awareness more easily. Adding successively more recent cases may permit capture of the exceptions and the more episodic, or routinized choices, the rules for which are less accessible to the expert.

RELIABILITY

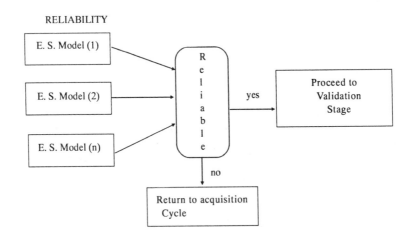

Figure 5.3. Establishing Reliability at the Multiple Model Stage

Where a decision-matrix is to be used to develop a skeleton of the expert system by inductive means, a **Jack-knife strategy** could be employed in which the system is induced n-1 times, where each case is in turn omitted from the development and subsequently used as a test case for determining validity in that particular cycle of development.

Where test cases are not available, or are few, exhaustive listing of all possible combinations may be helpful. These combinations might all be examined, or they might be sampled, or they might be used to provide statistics for simulation of smaller sets. Listing of all possible combinations is especially straightforward in small knowledge-based systems which are completely organized by class-inclusion. A spreadsheet is a useful way to create a decision matrix (or in more complicated expert systems, subsets of decision matrices). The ability of an expert system to arrive at the proper conclusion for each cell is a direct measure of its state of validity.

One potential finding is that the decision matrix approach tends to "test" the model with the same data from which the model as detected. Thus, the test is merely that of descriptive adequacy: Can the expert system parrot back the rules described in the spreadsheet? Another problem is that, for larger domains, it is not always possible to list all possibilities, much less run each one through a consultation with the expert system. Here sampling can be employed to insure that regions throughout the knowledge space are tested. Furthermore, the decision matrix approach can be impractical for systems of more than a few hundred rules.

Confidence factors especially require testing. Of course, if the expert system of which they are a part proves robust in the tests described in this chapter, there must be some merit to the system for manipulation of confidence factors and the values

VALIDATION CYCLE

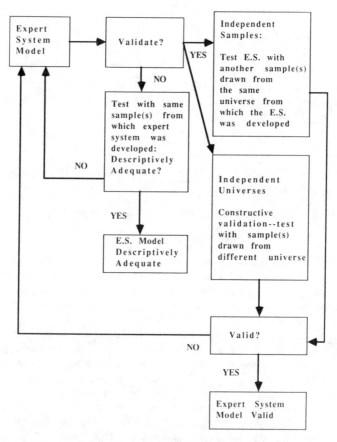

Figure 5.4. Validation Performance of Expert Systems

used; however, it would still be desirable to test them for sensitivity. Where tests cases are available, or an exceptionally patient expert will participate, it is useful to rerun the same data varying only one confidence factor each time, until and if the conclusion is changed. One or more confidence factors could also be tested by simulation, where each generated case is used to explore the sensitivity of the confidence factors for each rule or part of a rule. Since confidence factors can be embedded in antecedent conditions, consequent conditions, and combined or specified as the strength of the rule, each of these may be examined.

For any given expert system, exhaustive testing by simulation or test cases requires a heavy investment of time. Limited testing of critical components of the expert system, at each stage of the development cycle, can reduce total development time by catching errors at an early stage.

Independent Tests of Validity. Validity is the most important test of any expert system. Here we give several examples of research designs that permit validity of the model to be assessed. Even if the representation, or organization of knowledge, is syntactically correct, an expert system does not necessarily predict correct choices. We have argued that outcome-oriented statistical models, used in concert with more structural multivariate models, can enhance the predictive validity of an expert system. Such systems, in which weights are developed for the confidence factors from statistical forecasting methods, can both describe the organization of knowledge and predict behavior. To illustrate this approach we return to AI-MOMS, an example from medical anthropology. The goal was to predict the time when women would first present themselves for prenatal care. Thirty women were interviewed in this pilot study (Fisher et al., 1988; McKinney, 1987). A single investigator conducted a series of semistructured interviews on reasons for seeking prenatal care and wrote up field notes from them immediately afterward. Interviews had been conducted with the women within one to four days of their having first presented themselves for prenatal examination. Several investigators made independent codings of the notes for 26 variables, and a model was developed from the results. McKinney (1987) selected five variables from the original set, which had fewer than 20% individuals with missing data, a reliability coefficient greater than .7, and nonsignificant differences among the inter-coder mean scores. An adjusted r^2 of .8 was obtained using five reliable indicators.

Further analyses of the interview data illustrate the potential of combining expert systems with other statistical procedures in order to account for individual differences. Figure 5.5 presents two dimensions of a nonmetric multidimensional scaling of the data, with the criterion, Time of Presentation *omitted.* The numbers next to each point are the regression weights obtained when the number of weeks into the pregnancy are the dependent variables. The weights are the number of weeks the model predicts that presentation for prenatal care would be earlier (negative weights) or later (positive weights) than 25 weeks (the intercept).

As can be seen from Figure 5.5, there appears to be two vectors that could predict when prenatal care would be sought. The multidimensional scaling compares the *structure,* and the multiple regression helps identify the *direction* of the two vectors, which can be reconceptualized as a *paradigm* (see Table 5.1). The results were not self-evident. For instance, neither physicians nor anthropologists expected that encouragement by a female relative could lead to late presentation, although rereading the interviews showed that this was the case.

It was possible to create a very parsimonious expert system, AI-MOMS. A few deterministic rules, concerned with only two variables, one from each vector in Figure

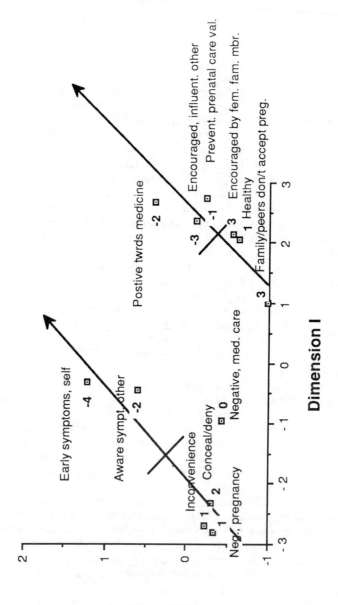

Figure 5.5. Nonmetric Multidimensional Scaling: Cognitive Factors

TABLE 5.1 Paradigmatic Representation of Dimensions of Multidimensional
Scaling with Time of Presentation for Prenatal Care

	Present Early	*Present Late*
Dimension I (INDIVIDUAL)	Early symptoms, self Aware symptoms, other	Conceal/deny pregnancy Negative toward pregnancy Inconvenient to present Negative toward medicine
Dimension II (SOCIAL)	Encouraged, influential other Positive toward medicine Previous prenatal care valuable	Encouraged, female family member Healthy Family/peers don't accept pregnancy

5.5 predict quite well whether presentation is early or late; the following rules are the
most important:

    Rule 1 **IF** Encouraged by Influential
          Other = yes,
        THEN present early
    Rule 2 **IF** Encouraged by Influential
          Other = no,
        THEN present late
    Rule 3 **IF** Encouraged by Influential
          Other = indeterminate
          (from interviews)
        AND Early Symptoms = yes,
        THEN present early
        ELSE present late.

From the *training* set of 17 cases, these few rules predict early vs. late presentation
88% correctly. For the eight *test* cases, seven out of eight are correctly predicted. The
single error is for a woman who presented at 22 weeks (the cutoff was somewhat
arbitrarily set at 20 weeks). More redundancy in the form of additional rules produces
a less elegant model but one perhaps more resistant, more robust in predicting
behavior in other samples.

    A second example illustrates another way validation might be approached, in this
case, where there was only one expert. Grading of compositions in freshman English
classes may be a highly subjective procedure; however, it would be desirable to know
the methods used by even one expert. Accordingly, an expert system was developed,
for the grading of a micro-theme assignment in English composition at a university,
with the idea that possibly it could be made available to the many teaching assistants
responsible for much of the teaching (Easterday, 1987). After development of the

system using the EXSYS shell, the original set of graded themes was used to test the system for reliability and validity.

Expert reliability was tested by having the same expert regrade 20 themes after one week. The reliability of the expert system was established the same way. Three persons — the original expert, a somewhat experienced teacher, and a student — each used the expert system to assign grades. Validity was assessed by comparing the prototype expert system grade with that assigned by the expert. Of particular interest was the finding that the student was able to assign grades that did not differ much more from the original expert-assigned grade than did the expert or the less-experienced teacher. In the few cases where the expert system grades differed by more than one letter grade from the grades given directly by the expert, careful study of these themes would probably permit the expert system to be refined in a future cycle of development.

A Typology of Validity. We recognize a series of kinds of validation according to their strength. The **weakest** form of validation involves exegesis with the expert until he or she finds the model "acceptable." By acceptable, we mean that the expert system performs in a manner that is congruent with the expectations of the expert or experts. An additional constraint might be that the logic of the expert system does not do violence to the intuition or private theory held by the expert.

At a minimum, **weak** validation is also necessary, but not sufficient; the expert system must obtain an acceptable level of performance with the test cases, if any, used to develop it. For instance, Guillet (1989) tested a very parsimonious model of crop management against the same data by which he obtained the model through preliminary induction. Naturally, these examples should fit. Weak validation is a guard against errors; it demonstrates that a model can explain back the data from which it was developed.

There are at least three levels of **strong** validation. (1) Previous choices or classifications available from recall or from records may be used for a test. Recall data have some problems for validation (Bernard et al., 1984); as time passes, they may trend toward the normative (Benfer, 1989), and where the recall cases are from the same expert(s) from which the system was developed, there is a lack of independence in the test. (2) Jack-knife, or other methods of testing the prediction of a particular case against a model developed from the remaining cases, may be used in the relatively rare instance in which the complete model can be produced inductively from a set of examples. This method might be used to test portions of the expert system that can be so represented. (3) Reserving test cases, which were not attended to in the development process, is essential. Where a model can be developed from one expert and tested against another's choices, we might say that there is good *inter-expert reliability.* Where the model can be tested with a new set of data and perform adequately, we might say that there is *model validity.* In the prenatal care example, AI-MOMS, the model was found to perform very well with a reserved set of data selected at random. All of the usual safeguards of scientific research are required;

random selection makes a stronger argument than selection of fortuitous cases. A blind test, where the user of the expert system in the test has not been associated with the development, also guards against bias.

Constructive validation is the strongest form of validation (Furbee and Benfer, 1989). In this case, the model is developed with a sample from one universe and is tested with a sample taken from a different but related universe. This is one of the strongest methods by which errors and inadequacies in a model can be determined. The AI-FORENS case (Benfer et al., 1990) offers an example of constructive validation. The model was created by the three investigators, working with the participating experts and with sample *os coxae* bones from collections in their own and the experts' laboratories. For validation, data were collected on 100 individual specimens of known sex and age in the Terry Collection at the Smithsonian Institution. To provide a blind test of constructive validation, these data were collected independently by a graduate student who was not involved in the development process and was, in fact, naive to expert systems.

Simulation is recommended to help the developer find unusually sensitive confidence intervals during development. However, simulations based on known or assumed properties of actual data may help form a picture of robustness, even if they do not provide a direct test of validation; i.e., the ability of an expert system to perform correctly with new examples. If relatively slight departures from the instances used to develop the system result in shifts in the final choices, then the validity of the system would be poor if it were to be tested with an independent sample.

In our experience, there is no substitute for reserving test cases, where they are available. Where possible, we recommend reserving two sets. The first, and smaller (and of lower quality if necessary), should be used to debug the last versions of the model. The second set should be reserved for a formal test of the expert system, its "clinical trial."

One can see, then, that validation is not a single event in the development of an expert system, but a part of each cycle of development (Figures 5.2-5.4). Inductive approaches are useful in expert systems only for beginning stages; they are especially appropriate to instances where the heart of the knowledge can be collected into a matrix form. Even advanced inductive programs still do not approach the human ability to deduce underlying rules. Deductive models are a better choice than inductive ones. They permit intermediate values and commonsense reasoning and also allow one to change previously reached conclusions on the basis of new evidence. They will allow confidence factors in antecedent conditions, in conclusions, and in the overall strength of the rule.

Expert systems mix various methods, an advantage that makes them more vulnerable than most models to being idiosyncratic, and so they must be validated with independent cases. The ability to predict new instances from the same universe successfully means that some degree of *validation* has been achieved; the ability to extend the model to related samples shows *constructive validation*.

How Expert Systems Can Improve Social Science

The contributions of social science methods and theory to expert systems have been emphasized throughout this book. However, we conclude by noting that expert systems may help social scientists address problems in creating cumulative knowledge from research.

Social science studies are often accused of showing a poor ability to accumulate knowledge, and so build directly on previous research (Rosenthal, 1984). Several reasons have been suggested why social science suffers more from these problems than do some other sciences. One is the inability to design true experiments where rejection of a null hypothesis must bear directly upon a specified alternative one. Another is the general inability to decide among competing explanations by studying point predictions of each where they are expected to differ. Finally, social science problems tend to be so complex that many theories do not produce hypotheses with sufficient specificity to permit their performance against competing ones to be evaluated. While the inductive problem identified by Hume has been addressed (Popper, 1972) in focusing on rejecting wrong hypotheses, the null hypothesis that there are no relations or effects is rarely the most informative one to reject in nonexperimental studies (see Henkel, 1976), and the entire falsificationist program has itself been called into question (e.g., Lakatos and Musgrave, 1970).

Expert systems fit easily into the basic scientific approach where the relations among assumptions are based upon rules or equations, and the relations among the objects are based upon empirical observation. By requiring that relations among antecedent conditions be formally stated as a series of rules, the scientist avoids advancing underdetermined theoretical schemes. The expert system will advise any user when there is no information for a particular combination of conditions. Used interactively, expert systems let the scientist continue to specify relations among conditions until satisfied that most or all conditions have been allowed for. Given enough conditions and rules as to their interrelationships as well as their function ultimately to predict some choice, it may be possible to work toward a social science equivalent of "point predictions," which we might call "overdetermined logic predictions."

Nonetheless, scientific knowledge cannot simply be reduced to analytical rules; patterns must be recognized. Objects or conditions in the world must be both recognized and evaluated. It has been suggested that human cognition involves preferences for patterns, which are represented as hierarchical structures, with heavy use of analogies in the formation of the representation. We will not discuss this latter condition here, although it is one to which linguists have devoted considerable attention in recent years (Lakoff, 1987).

Expert systems can be so rule-oriented that the human operator is used as the pattern recognition engine; that is, judgments of pattern are determined entirely by the user. We have suggested that statistical methods, such as multidimensional scaling, may be useful in making more objective these judgments. Patterns in the rules themselves are more naturally studied by representing the rules in an AI language.

Expert systems can hold considerable interest for social scientists, or humanists (Gardín, 1988), who need to make explicit the system of logic used to specify relationships. More important, by changing properties of the system, for example, by changing the method of manipulating confidence intervals, one can play "what if" games with the logic of the model. Looked at this way, expert systems may become the spreadsheet of scientific modeling of the logic of explanation.

Expert systems lie, perhaps a little uneasily, between the behaviorist and the linguistic (cognitive) approach to understanding knowledge. As Habermas (1988) notes, behaviorism identifies society with nature by reducing all action to behavior, whereas linguistics removes nature from society by placing social facts on the side of symbolic systems. Expert systems provide a method for social scientists to retain theoretical control over manipulation of symbols, while at the same time maintaining a connection with the empirical world by measuring success against the performance of the system in correctly predicting real-world choices. Thus, expert systems offer an explicit bridge between the world of ideas (commonly expressed as rules about choices) and the social and natural worlds.

APPENDIX
Expert System Shells, Artificial Intelligence Languages, and Sample Expert Systems

Shells

1st Class, 1st-Class Fusion, 1st-Class HT. A rule-based program with induction from examples, complete visual rule tree, and optimization of rules. Chaining rules for deep logical structures is awkward. Fairly easy to learn. Getting rules to work properly may be a bit tricky, particularly when you let the program help. Fusion and HT have easy access to Lotus and Dbase programs. HT includes hypertext. Overpriced.

    Company: AI Corp., 138 Technology Drive, Waltham, MA 02151; (617) 891-6500

    Price: Fusion $995-$2,000; HT $2,000, free run time

    Platforms: MS-DOS/IBM 512 RAM, MS-DOS 2.0+, two floppies or hard drive

VP-EXPERT. A rule-based program with hypertext, induction from examples, visual tree for rules fired in a session, no optimization of rules. Speedy, but interface is a bit awkward. Both forward- and backward-chaining are offered, and it can read and write both Lotus 1-2-3 and DBase files. Inexpensive, good value.

Company: Paperback Software International, 2830 Ninth St., Berkeley, CA 94710; (415) 644-2116

Price: $249, annual fee for run time $200; student version $39

Platforms: MS-DOS/IBM 512 RAM, MS-DOS 2.0+, two floppies or hard drive

Personal Consultant Easy, Personal Consultant Plus. A rule-based shell having both backward- and forward-chaining, relatively slow, easy to learn, and smooth-looking results. it is written in Scheme, a variant of LISP. It can read and write to DBase and read Lotus 1-2-3 files. It lacks hypertext, but the Plus version can provide object-oriented programming in Scheme. Can be difficult to modify and sacrifice programming control for simplicity.

Company: Texas Instruments, M/S 7722, P.O. Box 1444, Houston, TX 77251; (800) 527-3500

Prices: Easy $495; Personal Consultant Plus $2,950; $95 each for run time copies or $1,995 for unlimited distribution

Platforms: MS-DOS/IBM 512K RAM, MS-DOS 2.0+, two floppies or hard drive

KnowledgePro. A rule-based system with "topics" providing object-oriented frames as well. Permits both backward- and forward-chaining. Induction of rules from examples requires $99 related product. Has well-integrated hypertext capability, versatile language capable of list processing with many of the advantages of a powerful language, as opposed to a shell. Reads and writes DBase and Lotus 1-2-3 files. Written in LISP-like language.

Company: Knowledge Garden Inc., 473A Malden Bridge Rd., Nassau, NY 12123; (518) 766-3000

Price: $495, unlimited free run time; KnowledgePro Windows $700

Platforms: MS-DOS/IBM 512K RAM, MS-DOS 2.0+, two floppies or hard drive

ART-IM. A professional expert system development tool with a mouse and menu-driven interface, easily permits both rules and frames, powerful built-in language, efficient development and operation. Unfortunately, its prices place it beyond access for most social science applications.

Company: Inference Corporation, 5300 West Century Boulevard, Los Angeles, CA 90045; (213) 417-7997

Price: ART IM/MS-DOS first development copy $8,000; runtime $800 each

Platforms: MS-DOS/requires an AT or PS/2 compatible, DOS 3.x or higher, at least 2 MBytes of extended memory, and 6 MBytes of hard disk space just for the program. ART-IM is also available on IBM mainframes (MVS) and DEC hardware (VMS)

Level 5. A rule-based program with backward-chaining or forward-chaining. It includes a relatively powerful built-in language. Can read and write to DBase, but not to Lotus 1-2-3 files. Lacks rule induction, hypertext, and frames or objects. Available on multiple platforms.

Company: Information Builders, Inc., Level 5 Division, 1250 Broadway, New York, NY 10001; (212) 736-4333, (800) 444-4303

Price: $685; IBM version came copy-protected; $150 for each run time or $3,000 for unlimited number

Platforms: MS-DOS/IBM 512K RAM, MS-DOS 2.0+, two floppies or a hard drive

Also available on Macintosh, VAX, and IBM mainframes

EXSYS and EXSYS Professional. A rule-based system with forward- and backward-chaining. It lacks induction from examples, hypertext, or frames and its built-in rule editor requires some learning time. Includes a report facility; can call external programs.

Company: Expert System Development Package, EXSYS, Inc., P.O. Box 75158, Contract Station 14, Albuquerque, NM 87194

Price: EXSYS $395; EXSYS Professional $795; crippled student version $20; run time fee negotiable

Platforms: MS-DOS/IBM 512K RAM, MS-DOS 2.0+, two floppies or a hard drive

Intelligent Developer. Excellent debugging aids; relatively unconstrained developer interface; expert systems can be delivered as HyperCard stacks or with a supplied (and faster) compiler; good built-in database; can access others; good manual but overly brief; relatively buggy Version 1.0.

Company: Hyperpress Publishing Corp., and Dan Shafer, P.O. Box 8243, Foster city, CA 94404; (415) 345-5620

Price: $600 ($200 for academics); runtime free for 10 copies, one time fee of $50 for unlimited subsequent ones

Platforms: Macintosh, two floppies, hard drive and two megabytes of memory desirable for HyperCard development

Languages

TurboProlog. A nonstandard but very popular implementation of Prolog on IBM and MC/DOS machines, efficient and quick, with the nicely done Borland user interface using windows and pull-down menus. Excellent value for the price, but some users may find the exclusion of some Edinburgh-standard Prolog features to be a problem.

Company: Borland International, 1800 Green Hills Rd., P.O. Box 660001, Scotts Valley, CA 95066-0001; (408) 438-8400

Price: $149.95 ($44.90 educational price), no runtime fees for compiled programs

Platforms: MS-DOS/IBM 384K RAM, MS-DOS 2.0+

Allegro Common Lisp. An implementation of common LISP on the Macintosh. It is highly compatible with Franz LISP on Sun workstations, Vaxes, and even the Cray supercomputer. Like many LISP implementations, may require considerable memory for application.

Company: Coral Software Corp., P.O. Box 307, Cambridge, MA 02142; (800) 521-1027

Price: $600 plus shipping and handling (an educational discount is available). An additional $600 and "modest licensing fee" purchases a stand-alone application generator for distributing run-time copies to users

Platforms: Macintosh with 1MByte RAM

MuLISP-87. A solid implementation of LISP on MS/DOS machines including Common LISP functions, an object-oriented module, and graphics; very good tutorial introduction to LISP programming.

Company: SoftWarehouse, Inc., 3615 Harding Ave., Suite 505, Honolulu, HI 96816; (808) 734-5801

Price: $300 for interpreter, $400 for interpreter plus compiler (the latter permits free runtime versions)

Platforms: MS/DOS machine with at least 256KBytes of RAM

Small Talk/V Mac. A Macintosh implementation of SmallTalk, a classic object-oriented language. It includes the ability to use primitives from other languages and is compatible with the PC version.

Company: Digitalk, Inc., 9841 Airport Blvd., Los Angeles, CA 90045; (213) 645-1082

Price: $200

Platforms: Macintosh with 1.5MBytes of RAM and a hard disk. Also available on MS-DOS compatible machines

ALS Prolog. This is an implementation of Prolog available on Macintoshes, MS-DOS machines, and Sun workstations. It permits incremental compiling for speedier development. It generally follows the Edinburgh standard. In addition to the manual you will need a book on Prolog such as Clocksin and Mellish to understand its logic.

> **Company:** Applied Logic Systems, Inc., P.O. Box 90, University Station, Syracuse, NY 13210-0090; (315) 471-3900

> **Price:** Professional MS-DOS Version ($499), Personal MS-DOS Version ($299), Macintosh Version ($349), Sun Version ($4,200)

> **Platforms:** Macintosh/Plus, SE, or II with at least 1 MByte RAM. Also available for MS-DOS and Sun Workstations

Information Regarding Expert Systems Mentioned in This Book Available from:

1) The Idea Works, Inc., 100 N. Briarwood Ln., Columbia, MO 65202; (314) 445-4554.

2) Applied Expert System Research Group, c/o Prof. A. Hahn, The Dalton Research Center, University of Missouri-Columbia, Columbia, MO 65211.

NOTES

1. In this book, however, we will be relatively inclusive in discussing expert systems applications to the social sciences, because expert systems developed using artificial intelligence techniques are often implemented using more traditional languages such as C. The crucial element of expert systems for this book is that the programs address the kinds of problems commonly addressed by experts.

2. When speaking specifically about the knowledge in a data base, a distinction is often made between *explicit* knowledge and *implicit* knowledge that parallels that between *public* and *private* knowledge in the real world.

3. For an example of PROLOG, look ahead in this chapter.

4. These distinctions derive from accommodation of two fundamental relations among elements, the *paradigmatic* and the *syntagmatic*. A paradigm is the cartesian product of all possible attributes of a system (Conklin, 1961; Degerman, 1972). The result is easily visualized as a matrix or spreadsheet, a form we will recommend as useful for managing rules during development of an expert system. Since any serious expert system will have many rules, they

84

must be managed in some way, and a spreadsheet format is useful for a variety of reasons. For example:

If	A	B	A & B	A or B
Then	x	y	y	?
Else	?	z	?	?

alerts the expert system developer of areas where there are no applicable rules available at each stage of the process. A paradigmatic relation holds among members of a set. On the other hand, a syntagmatic relation holds across sets in a sequence. In a sequence like "Susan likes tea," "Susan" has a paradigmatic relation with other members of a set that might occupy the subject position in this sentence (e.g., "Mildred," "Bill," etc.). The relations holding across words are syntagmatic ones, so in the example above, "Susan" has syntagmatic relations with "likes" and "tea," as indeed those two words do with "Susan" and with one another. The difference in paradigmatic and syntagmatic relations fits well the expert system use of **If . . . Then** structures to define syntactic and contextual relations.

5. These backward-chaining and forward-chaining forms of operation may be compared with conventions in the operation of parser programs and in the operation of linguistic rules. With respect to parser programs, a backward-chaining expert system is analogous in operation to a top-down parser program. The operation of forward-chaining expert systems is analogous to that of bottom-up parsers. In linguistic terms, backward-chaining reasons from a known structural change (goal, outcome) to find the appropriate structural description (premise) that describes the change. Backward-chaining rules are unordered and may be said to retrodict in terms of their mode of operation. On the other hand, forward-chaining rules, which are always ordered, seek conclusions from premises.

6. See Appendix for companies and addresses of expert system shells mentioned in this book.

7. The expert already had a fairly explicitly articulated set of general categories and rules for decisions. But the knowledge acquisition program was designed to elicit such categories and rules at a much slower rate and in a different sequence based on cases. We got only part way into the program, when the expert became so frustrated she refused to proceed. We abandoned this approach.

8. These terms were coined from a familiar distinction used in the study of the sound systems of languages. **Phonetic** refers to the description of the individual sounds of a language regardless of their groupings into sound patterns perceptually and cognitively by the speakers of that language, whereas **phonemic** refers to the units (groupings of phonetic elements) of sound as they participate in the sound pattern of a particular language. The same set of sounds (phonetic entities) may exist in different languages but be grouped by each into different phonemic entities. For example, both English and Korean have these three phonetic sounds, $[p^h,p,b]$, and both group them into two phonemes; however, English groups $[p^h,p]$ into the phoneme /p/ and [b] into phoneme /b/, whereas Korean groups them thusly: $[p^h]$ into phoneme $/p^h/$ and [p,b] into phoneme /b/. The use of the emic/etic distinction in anthropology resembles the difference that sociologists draw between **interpretive** and **objective** approaches.

9. The balanced incomplete block design method (Burton and Nerlove, 1976) is described in Bernard (1988) and in Weller and Romney (1988: 36-37, 499-55).

10. A simple, well documented MS-DOS program, ANTHROPAC, aids in gathering and scoring this and other ethnosemantic procedures. It is for sale for a nominal fee of $25 from Steve Borghatti, Dept. of Anthropology, University of California, Berkeley.

11. STELLA (High Performance Systems, 13 Dartmouth College Highway, Lynne, NY 03768) is a relatively inexpensive and easy-to-use simulation program for examining portions of an expert system's sensitivity to specific ranges of confidence factors.

REFERENCES

AIKENS, J. (1983) "Prototypical Knowledge for Expert Systems." Artificial Intelligence, 20: 163-210.

ALDENDERFER, M. S., & BLASHFIELD, R. K. (1984) Cluster Analysis. Beverly Hills, CA: Sage.

ALLEN, J., & PERRAULT, C. (1980) "Analyzing Intention in Utterances." Artificial Intelligence 16: 143-178.

ANDERSON, J. R. (1983) The Architecture of Cognition. Cambridge, MA: Harvard University Press.

ANDREWS, F., KLEM, L., DAVIDSON, T., O'MALLEY, P., & RODGERS, W. (1981) A Guide for Selecting Statistical Techniques for Analyzing Social Science Data (2nd ed.). Ann Arbor, MI: University of Michigan.

ARABIE, P., CARROLL, J. D., & DESSARBO, W. S. (1987) Three-Way Scaling and Clustering. Beverly Hills, CA: Sage.

BANERJEE, S. (1986) "The Reproduction of Social Structures." Journal of Conflict Resolution 30: 221-252.

BENFER, R. A., Jr. (1988) "Individual Differences in Expert Systems with Behavioral Implications." Paper presented at the annual meeting of the American Anthropological Association.

BENFER, R. A., Jr. (1989) "Individual Differences in Rule-based Systems of Knowledge with Behavioral Implications." Anthropological Quarterly 52: 69-82.

BENFER, R. A., Jr., & FURBEE, L. (1989a) "Procrustes Analysis of Individual Configurations: Patterns and Axes Similarities." Journal of Quantitative Anthropology 1: 65-80.

BENFER, R. A., Jr., & FURBEE, L. (1989b) "Knowledge Acquisition in the Peruvian Andes." AI Expert 4: 22-29.

BENFER, R. A., Jr., FURBEE, L., & BRENT, E. E., Jr. (1990) "AI-FORENS: A Knowledge-Based System for Age and Sex Determinations from the Os Coxae." Paper presented to the American Academy of Forensic Sciences.

BELL, J., & HARDIMAN, R. (1989) "The Third Role — The Naturalistic Knowledge Engineer," pp. 49-85 in D. Diaper (ed.) Knowledge Elicitation. New York: Wiley.

BERNARD, H. R., KILLWORTH, P. D., KRONENFELD, D., & SAILER, L. (1984) "The Problem of Informant Accuracy: The Validity of Retrospective Data." Annual Review of Anthropology 13: 495-517.

BERNARD, H. R. (1988) Research Methods in Cultural Anthropology. Newbury Park, CA: Sage.

BINIK, Y. M., SERVAN-SCHREIBER, D., FREIWALD, S., & HALL, K. S. (1988) "Intelligent Computer-Based Assessment and Psychotherapy: An Expert System for Sexual Dysfunction." Journal of Neurological and Mental Disorders 176: 387-400.

BLANK, G. (1989) "Modeling Social Theory Through Expert Systems." Paper delivered at the annual meeting of the American Sociological Association.

BLUM, R. (1984) "Discovery, Confirmation and Incorporation of Causal Relationships from a Large Time-Oriented Clinical Data Base: The RX Project," pp. 307-311 in W. Clancey, and E. Short (eds.) Readings in Medical Artificial Intelligence. Reading, MA: Addison-Wesley.

BOBROW, D. B., SYLVAN, D. A., & RIPLEY, B. (1986) "Japanese Supply Security: A Computational Model." Paper delivered at the International Studies Association.

BOSTER, J. S. (1986) "Exchange of Varieties and Information Between Aguaruna Cultivators." American Anthropologist 88: 428-436.

BOSTER, J. S. (1987) "Agreement Between Biological Classification Systems is not Dependent on Cultural Transmission." American Anthropologist 89: 914-919.

BREIMAN, L., FRIEDMAN, J. H., & OLSHEN, R. A. (1984) Classification and Regression Trees. Belmont, CA: Wadsworth International Group.

BRENT, E. (1986) "Knowledge-Based Systems: A Qualitative Formalism." Qualitative Sociology 9: 256-282.

BRENT, E. (1988a) Statistical Navigator. Columbia, MO: The Idea Works, Inc.

BRENT, E. (1988b) "Statistical Expert Systems: An Example." Journal of Statistical Computation and Simulation 27: 137-151.

BRENT, E. (1989a) "Is There a Role for Artificial Intelligence in Sociological Theorizing?", pp. 129-137 in G. Blank, J. McCartney, and E. Brent (eds.) New Technology in Sociology: Practical Applications in Research and Work. New Brunswick, NJ: Transaction.

BRENT, E. (1989b) "Designing Social Science Research with Expert Systems." Anthropological Quarterly 62: 121-130.

BRENT, E. (1989c) "Building Expert Systems to Assist in Designing and Conducting Research: Simulations Based on Symbolic Reasoning." Paper delivered at the annual meeting of the Midwest Sociological Society.

BRENT, E. (1989d) "Using Expert Systems to Design Social Science Research." Paper delivered at the annual meeting of the Decision Sciences Institute.

BRENT, E. (1989e) Measurement and Scaling Strategist. Columbia, MO: The Idea Works, Inc.

BRENT, E. (1989f) Data Collection Selection. Columbia, MO: The Idea Works, Inc.

BRENT, E. (1990) "Sociological Reasoning with a Computer." Paper delivered at the Advanced Computing in the Social Sciences Conference.

BRENT, E., RUDE, D., & EBERT, R. (1986) "A Comparison of an Expert Rule Induction System with Traditional Multivariate Regression Analysis." Paper delivered at the annual meeting of the Decision Sciences Institute.

BRENT, E., SPENCER, J., & SCOTT, J. (1988) EX-SAMPLE. Columbia, MO: The Idea Works, Inc.

BRENT, E., GLAZIER, J., JAMTGAARD, K., WETZEL, E., HALL, P., DALECKI, M., & BAH, A. (1989a) "ERVING: A Program to Teach Sociological Reasoning from the Dramaturgical Perspective." Teaching Sociology 17: 38-48.

BRENT, E., & MIRIELLI, E. (1989) Designer Research. Columbia, MO: The Idea Works, Inc.

BRENT, E., SCOTT, J., & SPENCER, J. (1989b) "EX-SAMPLE: An Expert System Program to Assist in Determining Sample Size." Social Science Computer Review 7: 314-319.

BRENT, E., & ANDERSON, R. E. (1990) Computer Applications in the Social Sciences. New York: McGraw-Hill.

BRENT, R., BRENT, E. E., PHILLIPS, R., GUPTA, M., & RAY, S. (In review) "Safety Concerns of Housing for Older Adults." Housing and Society.

BUCHANAN, B. G. (1985) Knowledge-Based Systems: Guidelines for Problem Selection, Knowledge Acquisition, Validation. Texas Instruments Satellite Teleconference, November 13.

BUCHANAN, B. G., BARSTOW, D., BECHTEL, R., BENNET, J., CLANCEY, W., KULIKOWSKI, C., MITCHELL, T. M., & WATERMAN, D. A. (1983) "Constructing an Expert System," pp. 127-168 in F. Hayes-Roth, D. A. Waterman, and D. B. Lenat (eds.) Building Expert Systems. Reading, MA: Addison-Wesley.

BURTON, M. L., & NERLOVE, S. B. (1976) "Balanced Designs for Triads Tests: Two Examples from English." Social Science Research 5: 247-267.

CANCIAN, F. (1963) "Informant Error and Native Prestige Ranking in Zinacantan." American Anthropologist 65: 1068-1075.

CARLEY, K. (1988) "Formalizing the Social Expert's Knowledge." Sociological Methods & Research 17: 165-232.

CHANDRASEKAREN, B. (1988) "Towards a Taxonomy of Problem Solving Types." AI-Magazine 4: 9-17.

CIMBALA, S. J. (1987) Artificial Intelligence and National Security. Lexington, MA: D.C. Heath.

CLOCKSIN, W., & MELLISH, C. (1984) Programming in PROLOG (2nd ed.) Berlin: Springer-Verlag.

COHEN, J. (1960) "A Coefficient of Agreement for Nominal Scales." Educational and Psychological Measurement 20: 37-46.

COHEN, J. (1968) "Weighted Kappa: Nominal Scale Agreement with Provision for Scaled Disagreement or Partial Credit." Psychological Bulletin 70: 213-220.

COLBY, B. N. (1975) "Culture Grammars." Science 187: 913-919.

CONKLIN, H. C. (1961) "Lexicographic Treatment of Folk Taxonomies." International Journal of Anthropological Linguistics 28: 119-142.

DEGERMAN, R. I. (1972) "The Geometric Representation of Some Simple Structures," pp. 193-211 in A. K. Romney, R. N. Shepard, and S. B. Nerlove (eds.) Multidimensional Scaling (Vol. 1.). New York: Seminar Press.

DIAPER, D. (1989) Knowledge Elicitation: Principles, Techniques and Applications. Chichester, England: Ellis Horwood Ltd.

DURBROW, E. H. (1989) "Expert Systems as Tools for Managing Ethnographic Research." Paper presented to the annual meeting of the American Anthropology Association.

EASTERDAY, T. (1987) "An Expert System for Evaluating English Composition Assignments." Undergraduate Honors Thesis, Linguistics Program, University of Missouri-Columbia.

FEIGENBAUM, E. A. (1977) "The Art of Artificial Intelligence: Themes and Case Studies of Knowledge Engineering." IJCAI 5: 1014-1029.

FISHER, M. J., EWIGMAN, B., CAMPBELL, J., BENFER, R. A., FURBEE, L., & ZWEIG, S. (1988) "Factors Influencing Women to Seek Prenatal Care." Paper delivered to the 16th annual meeting of the North American Primary Care Research Group.

FLEISS, J. L. (1981) Statistical Methods for Rates and Proportions, 2nd ed. New York: Wiley.

FLEISS, J. L., COHEN, J., and EVERITT, B. S. (1969) "Large Sample Standard Errors of Kappa and Weighted Kappa." Psychological Bulletin 72: 323-327.

FRANZOSI, R. (1989) "From Words to Numbers: A Generalized and Linguistics-Based Coding Procedure for Collecting Textual Data," pp. 263-299 in C. C. Clogg (ed.) Sociological Methodology 1989. Oxford: Basil Blackwell.

FURBEE, L. (1987) "A Curer Consensus." Paper presented to the Society for Medical Anthropology, American Anthropological Association Meetings.

FURBEE, L. (1989) "A Folk Expert System: Soils Classification in the Colca Valley, Peru." Anthropological Quarterly 62: 83-102.

FURBEE, L., & BENFER, R. A. (1983) "Cognitive and Geographic Maps: Study of Individual Variation among Tojolabal Mayans." American Anthropologist 85: 305-334.

FURBEE, L., & BENFER, R. A. (1989) Validation in Expert Systems. Paper presented to the annual meeting of the American Anthropological Association.

FURBEE, L., & SANDOR, J. (1990) "Articulating Folk and Western Scientific Classification of Soils in the Colca Valley, Peru." Paper presented to the 18th Annual Midwest Conference on Andean and Amazonian Archaeology and Ethnohistory.

GARDÍN, J.-C. (1988) Artificial Intelligence and Expert Systems. Chichester, England: Ellis Horwood Ltd.

GARSON, G. D. (1987) "The Role of Inductive Expert Systems Generators in the Social Science Research Process." Social Science Microcomputer Review 5: 11-24.

GARSON, G. D. (1989) "Computer Simulation, Artificial Intelligence, and Political Science," pp. 25-46 in G. D. Garson and S. S. Nagel (eds.) Advances in Social Science and Computers. Greenwich, CT: JAI Press.

GEOGHEGAN, W. H. (1971) "Information Processing Systems in Culture," in P. Kay (ed.) Explorations in Mathematical Anthropology. Cambridge: The MIT Press.

GLYMOUR, C., SCHEINES, R., SPIRTES, P., & KELLY, K. (1987) Discovering Causal Structure. New York: Academic Press.

GOFFMAN, E. (1959) The Presentation of Self in Everyday Life. New York: Doubleday.

GOLDSTEIN, R. (1989) "Power and Sample Size via MS/PC-DOS Computers." American Statistician 43: 253-260.

GUILLET, D. (1989) "A Knowledge-based Systems Model of Native Soil Management." Anthropological Quarterly 62: 57-58.

HABERMAS, J. (1988) On the Logic of the Social Sciences. Cambridge, MA: MIT Press.

HART, A. (1986). Knowledge Acquisition for Expert Systems. New York: McGraw-Hill.

HAUX, R. (1986). Expert Systems in Statistics. Stuttgart: Gustav Fisher.

HAYES-ROTH, F. D., WATERMAN, D. A., & LENAT, D. B. (1983) "An Overview of Expert Systems," pp. 3-30 in F. Hayes-Roth, D. A. Waterman, and D. B. Lenat (eds.) Building Expert Systems. Reading, MA: Addison-Wesley.

HEDLUND, J. L., VIEWEG, B. W., & CHO, D. W. (1987) "Computer Consultation for Emotional Crises: An Expert System for Non-Experts." Computers in Human Behavior 3: 109-127.

HEDLUND, J. L., & VIEWEG, B. W. (1988) Mental Health Computing: Selected Bibliography. Columbia, MO: University of Missouri.

HEISE, D., & LEWIS, E. M. (1988) Introduction to ETHNO. Raleigh, NC: National Collegiate Software Clearinghouse.

HENKEL, R. E. (1976) Tests of Significance. Newbury Park, CA: Sage.

HOFFMAN, R. A. (1987) "The Problem of Extracting the Knowledge of Experts from the Perspective of Experimental Psychology." AI Magazine 8: 53-64.

HOFMEISTER, A. M., & LUBKE, M. M. (1988) "Expert Systems: Implications for the Diagnosis and Treatment of Learning Disabilities." Learning Disability Quarterly 11: 287-291.

HUDSON, V. M. (1987) "Using a Rule-Based Production System to Estimate Foreign Policy Behavior," pp. 109-131 in S. Cimbala (ed.) Artificial Intelligence and National Security. Lexington, MA: Lexington Books.

HUTCHINS, E. (1980) Culture and Inference: A Trobriand Case Study. Cambridge, MA: Harvard University Press.

JACKSON, E. (1987) Predicting Treatment at Home or in a Clinic for the Herding Villagers of Callalli, Peru. Manuscript, School of Nursing, University of Missouri, Columbia.

JOHNSON, A. (1980) "Ethnoecology and Planting Practices in a Swidden Agricultural System (Brazil)," in D. Brokensha, D. M. Warren, and O. Werner (eds.) New York: University Press of America.

KAW, M. (1986) "Testing a Model of Soviet Conflict Involvement Behavior." Paper Delivered at the annual meeting of the Midwest Political Science Association.

KEARNEY, M. (1984) World View, Novato: Chandler and Sharp.

KEMPTON, W. (1978) "Category Grading and Taxonomic Relations: A Mug Is a Sort of a Cup." American Ethnologist 5: 44-65.

KIPPEN, J. (1988) "On the Uses of Computers in Anthropological Research." Current Anthropology 29: 317-320.

KRUSKAL, J. B., & WISH, M. (1978) Multidimensional Scaling. Newbury Park, CA: Sage.

LAKATOS, I., & MUSGRAVE, A. (1970) Criticism and the Growth of Knowledge. Cambridge: Cambridge University Press.

LAKOFF, G. (1987) Women, Fire, and Dangerous Things: What Categories Reveal about the Mind. Chicago: University of Chicago Press.

LANE, R. (1986) "Artificial Intelligence and the Political Construction of Reality: The Case of James E. Carter." Paper delivered at the annual meeting of the American Political Science Association.

LENAT, D. B., DAVIS, R., DOYLE, J., GENESERTH, M., GOLDSTEIN, I., & SCHROBE, H. (1983) "Reasoning about Reasoning," pp. 219-240 in F. Hayes-Roth, D. A. Waterman, and D. B. Lenat (eds.) Building Expert Systems. Reading, MA: Addison-Wesley.

LEWIS-BECK, M. (1980) Applied Regression. Newbury Park, CA: Sage.

LORGE, I., & SOLOMON, H. (1960) "Group and Individual Performance in Problem Solving Related to Previous Exposure to Problem, Level of Aspiration, and Group Size." Behavioral Science 5: 23-38.

MAJESKI, S. J. (1987) "A Recommendation Model of War Initiation: The Plausibility and Generalizability of General Cultural Rules," pp. 61-86 in S. Cimbala (ed.) Artificial Intelligence and National Security. Lexington, MA: Lexington Books.

McKINNEY, G. (1987) "A Model for Predicting the Initial Presentation of Pregnant Women for Prenatal Care." Master's thesis, University of Missouri-Columbia.

MILTON, S. (1986) "A Sample Size Formula for Multiple Regression Studies." Public Opinion Quarterly 50: 112-118.

MINSKY, M. (1975) "A Framework for Representing Knowledge," pp. 211-279 in P. Winston (ed.) The Psychology of Computer Vision. New York: McGraw-Hill.

MOORE, B. (1966) The Social Origins of Dictatorship and Democracy: The Lord and The Peasant in the Making of the Modern World. Boston: Beacon Press.

NEGOITA, C. V. (1985) Expert Systems and Fuzzy Systems. Menlo Park, CA: Benjamin/Cummings Publishing Company, Inc.

NG, K.-C., & ABRAMSON, B. (1990) "Uncertainty Management in Expert Systems." IEEE Expert 5: 29-47.

O'DONNELL, G. (1973) Bureaucratic Authoritarianism and Modernization. Berkeley: University of California Press.

O'KEEFE, R. (1986) "Simulation and Expert Systems: A Taxonomy and Some Examples," Simulation 46: 10-16.

OVERBY, M. A. (1987) "Psyxpert: An Expert System Prototype for Aiding Psychiatrists in the Diagnosis of Psychotic Disorders." Computers in Biology and Medicine 1: 383.

POGGIE, J., Jr. (1972) "Toward Quality Control in Key Informant Data." Human Organization 31: 23-30.

POPPER, K. R. (1972) Objective Knowledge: an Evolutionary Approach. Oxford: Clarendon Press.

POSNER, M. I. (1990) The Foundations of Cognitive Science. Cambridge, MA: MIT Press.

RANDALL, R. (1976) "How Tall is a Taxonomic Tree: The Evidence for Dwarfism." American Ethnologist 3: 543-553.

READ, D., & BEHRENS, C. (1989) "Modeling Folk Knowledge as Expert Systems." Anthropological Quarterly 62: 107-120.

REYNOLDS, H. T. (1977) The Analysis of Cross-Classifications. New York: Free Press.

ROMNEY, A. K., WELLER, S. C., & BATCHEIDER, W. H. (1988) "Culture as Consensus: A Theory of Informant Accuracy." American Anthropologist 88: 313-338.

ROSCH, E. (1978) "Principles of Categorization," pp. 27-71 in E. Rosch, and B. Lloyd (eds.) Cognition and Categorization. Hillsdale, NJ: Lawrence Erlbaum Associates.

ROSENTHAL, R. (1984) Meta-Analytic Procedures for Social Research. Newbury Park, CA: Sage.

ROSE, M. D., & ROMNEY, A. K. (1979) "Cognitive Pluralism or Individual Differences: A Comparison of Alternative Models of American English Kin Terms." American Ethnologist 6: 752-762.

SANDOR, J. (1989) "Investigation of Agricultural Soils at Lari, Colca Valley, Peru," in D. Guillet, (ed.) Cognitive and Behavioral Studies of Soil Management in Peru. Report to the National Science Foundation.

SCHRODT, P. A. (1989) "Artificial Intelligence and Formal Models of International Behavior," pp. 113-127 in G. Blank, J. McCartney, and E. Brent (eds.) New Technology in Sociology: Practical Applications in Research and Work. New Brunswick, NJ: Transaction.

SEAR, A. M. (1988) "An Expert System for Determining Medicaid Eligibility." Journal of Medical Systems 12: 275-283.

SHANGRAW, R. F., Jr. (1987) "Knowledge Acquisition, Expert Systems, and Public Management Decisions." Social Science Microcomputer Review 5: 163-173.

SHELLY, A., & SIBERT, E. (1986) "Using Logic Programming to Facilitate Qualitative Data Analysis." Qualitative Sociology 9: 145-161.

SIMMEL, G. (1955) Conflict and the Web of Group Affiliations. New York: Free Press.

SKOCPOL, T. (1979) States and Social Revolutions. London: Cambridge University Press.

SLEEMAN, D., & BROWN, J. S. (1982) Intelligent Tutoring Systems. New York: Academic Press.

SPRADLEY, J. P. (1979) The Ethnographic Interview. London: Holt, Rinehart and Winston.

SYLVAN, D., & GLASSNER, B. (1985) A Rationalist Methodology for the Social Sciences. Oxford, England: Basil Blackwell.

TANAKA, A. (1984) "Chapter 11," in D. A. Sylvan and S. Chan (eds.) Foreign Policy Decision Making: Perception, Cognition, and Artificial Intelligence. New York: Praeger.

TAFT, D. K. (1988) "SSA Tests AI's Ability to Solve Routine Problems." Government Computer News 7: 20.

THORSAN, S., & SYLVAN, D. A. (1982) "Counterfactuals and the Cuban Missile Crisis." International Studies Quarterly 26: 539-571.

TSCHUDI, F. (1988) "Matrix Representation of Expert Systems." AI Expert 3: 44-53.

WATERMAN, D. A. (1986) A Guide to Expert Systems. Reading, MA: Addison-Wesley.

WATERMAN, D. A., & HAYES-ROTH, F. (1978) Pattern-Directed Inference Systems. New York: Academic Press.

WEBSTER, W. (1989) Simulation and AI, 1989. San Diego, CA: The Society for Computer Simulation International.

WEISS, S., KERN, K., KULIKOWSKI, C., & USEHOLD, M. (1981) A Guide to the Use of the EXPERT Consultation System. Department of Computer Science, Rutgers University.

WELLER, S. C., & ROMNEY, A. K. (1988) Systematic Data Collection. Newbury Park, CA: Sage.

WERNER, O., & SCHOEPFLE, G. M. (1987) Systematic Fieldwork (2 volumes). Newbury Park, CA: Sage.

WINOGRAD, T. (1972) Understanding Computers: A New Foundation for Design. Reading, MA: Addison-Wesley.

WINSTON, P., & HORN, B. (1985) LISP (2nd ed.). Reading, MA: Addison-Wesley.

ABOUT THE AUTHORS

The three authors are members of the Board of Directors of the Applied Expert Systems Research Group of the University of Missouri-Columbia.

ROBERT A. BENFER, JR. (Ph.D., Texas-Austin, 1967) is Professor of Anthropology at the University of Missouri-Columbia, and an Associate of I.D. Associates, a consulting firm. A methodologist, he has long been interested in the articulation of quantitative methods with qualitative means of representation for conceptual organization in the social and biological sciences. He has published widely on computer applications for anthropology, including archaeology, biological anthropology, forensic anthropology, and ethnology.

EDWARD E. BRENT, JR. (Ph.D., Minnesota, 1976) is Professor of Sociology and Adjunct Professor of Computer Science at the University of Missouri-Columbia and President of The Idea Works, Inc., a company specializing in the development of expert systems for the design and conduct of research. He is first author of *Computer Applications in the Social Sciences,* by McGraw-Hill; co-editor of *New Technology in Sociology: Practical Applications in Research and Work,* by Transaction Press; and Chair of the Microcomputing Section of the American Sociological Association. His research interests are applications of expert systems in the social sciences and the impact of computers on the practice of science.

LOUANNA FURBEE (Ph.D., Chicago, 1974), a linguistic and cognitive anthropologist, is Professor of Anthropology at the University of Missouri-Columbia and an Associate of I.D. Associates. She has long been interested in computer applications in linguistic anthropology: Her Tojolabal-Maya Text and Dictionary Project, 1976-1980 (*Tojolabal-Maya English Dictionary,* 1981, and *Tojolabal-Maya Text Concordance,* 1981) was an early example of computer-assisted lexicography for an American Indian language. More recently, she has been concerned with knowledge acquisition in expert systems development and in the construction of folk expert systems.

DATE DUE	BORROWER'S NAME	ROOM NUMBER
JUL 13 '94	M. Enright	16-R
AUG 5 '94	D. Danas	27-E